Methodology in Neuropsycholog Assessment

Methodology in Neuropsychological Assessment: An Interpretative Approach to Guide Clinical Practice provides practical and methodological guidance for neuropsychologists working with people with brain lesions or brain dysfunctions. The textbook underlines the principles that can be used to guide clinicians in recognizing and interpreting signs and symptoms while enabling a complete neuropsychological assessment through a series of well-defined steps. The text provides a detailed methodological approach towards neuropsychological tools, with guidance on how to select the right test and how to interpret the outcome, which can act as a primer for a clinician through every step of the assessment in a coherent and reasoned way.

The textbook presents an exhaustive discussion of the varied tools that a clinician can employ to complete a rigorous and consistent neuropsychological assessment. It guides the reader from the first step of collecting the personal history of the examinee – the anamnesis – to the selection of suitable psychometric tests and scoring, which is accordingly integrated to formulate the neuropsychological diagnosis and write up the neuropsychological report. Chapters also include coverage of the neuropsychological interview with the examinee and their family and the probability of identifying a disorder with a neuropsychological assessment. The authors have further included a series of detailed and explanatory clinical cases from their experience to expand upon the evaluation process.

The textbook is valuable reading for students in clinical neuropsychology who are learning to carry out neuropsychological evaluations as well as clinicians who are seeking to develop a more comprehensive approach towards perform a thorough neuropsychological assessment.

Sara Mondini, PhD, is a Professor of Clinical Neuropsychology and Neuropsychological Assessment at the University of Padua, Italy. She has long practice in clinical neuropsychology and has published numerous scientific papers on clinical neuropsychological pathologies like dementia and aphasia along with contributing to the development of cognitive tests.

Marinella Cappelletti, PhD, Neuropsychologist and Cognitive Neuroscientist is a Reader in the Psychology Department at Goldsmiths, University of London, UK. She initially trained in neuropsychology at the University of Padua, Italy, and later combined it with experimental psychology and neuroimaging methods during her doctoral and postdoctoral studies in the UK and US.

Giorgio Arcara has a degree in Psychology, a PhD in Psychobiology, and a post-graduate master in clinical neuropsychology. He has held a particular interest in the methodology in neuropsychology, and has authored numerous articles and contributions on neuropsychological test development. He further holds a coordination position in a research-oriented hospital.

Methodology in Neuropsychological Assessment

An Interpretative Approach to Guide Clinical Practice

**Sara Mondini,
Marinella Cappelletti,
and Giorgio Arcara**

Routledge
Taylor & Francis Group

LONDON AND NEW YORK

First published 2023
by Routledge
4 Park Square, Milton Park, Abingdon, Oxon OX14 4RN

and by Routledge
605 Third Avenue, New York, NY 10158

Routledge is an imprint of the Taylor & Francis Group, an informa business

British Library Cataloguing-in-Publication Data
A catalogue record for this book is available from the British Library

Library of Congress Cataloging-in-Publication Data
Names: Mondini, Sara, author. | Cappelletti, Marinella, author. |
   Arcara, Giorgio, 1982- author.
Title: Methodology in neuropsychological assessment :
   an interpretative approach to guide clinical practice /
   Sara Mondini, Marinella Cappelletti, Giorgio Arcara.
Description: Abingdon, Oxon : New York, NY : Routledge,
   2023. | Includes bibliographical references and index. |
   Identifiers: LCCN 2022010563 (print) | LCCN 2022010564
   (ebook) | ISBN 9781032049311 (hardback) | ISBN
   9781032049298 (paperback) | ISBN 9781003195221 (ebook)
Subjects: MESH: Neuropsychological Tests |
   Neuropsychology--methods | Interview, Psychological--
   methods | Neurocognitive Disorders--diagnosis |
   Psychometrics--methods
Classification: LCC 616.8/0475 (print) | LCC 616.8/0475
   (ebook) | NLM WL 141.5.N46 | DDC 616.8/0475--dc23/
   eng/20220606
LC record available at https://lccn.loc.gov/2022010563
LC ebook record available at https://lccn.loc.gov/2022010564

ISBN: 978-1-032-04931-1 (hbk)
ISBN: 978-1-032-04929-8 (pbk)
ISBN: 978-1-003-19522-1 (ebk)

DOI: 10.4324/9781003195221

Typeset in Bembo
by KnowledgeWorks Global Ltd.

Contents

An introduction to methodology in neuropsychology

The present book aims to provide: 1) a practical description of a rational Interpretative Approach that can be used to structure a neuropsychological assessment; 2) suggestions to improve the reasoning process that occurs during the assessment, starting from the initial meeting with the examinee to the final diagnosis.

This is not the first book addressing and proposing a methodology in clinical neuropsychology, and the interested reader is referred to other books that largely cover this topic (e.g., Lezak, 2014, Russel, 2011, Goldstein & Incagnoli, 1997). However, this book is novel in a number of ways which can be better appreciated by examining the recent advances in clinical neuropsychology.

Traditional neuropsychology following Binet's psychometric tests and post-war assessments aiming to identify brain damage in soldiers and veterans is based on several theoretical approaches often reflected in different clinical concepts and classifications.

For example, the 1950s' Boston Process approach (White & Rose, 1997), highlighted the importance of investigating performance in a test, as well as the 'process' used to perform the test. The Halstead-Reitan Battery, again from the 1950s, suggested instead the importance of investigating patterns of impairment from tests composing a fixed battery (Reed & Reed, 1997). More recent approaches instead provide a methodological rather than theoretical guidance, but with no indication of diagnostic reasoning during the assessment. For instance, this is the case of Lezak's descriptive methodological approach (2012, last edition) and Russel's (2011) methodological suggestion of the importance of formal, comprehensive, and automated test-batteries.

Collectively, these and other proposals established the foundations of the neuropsychological assessment, but there is still a disconnection between theoretical and methodological proposals and the current clinical practice. Our Interpretative Approach aims to fill this gap. It also expands the traditional in-person neuropsychological assessment with more technological and remote approaches.

The book is inspired by our original text "Semeiotics and Neuropsychological Diagnosis" by Mondini, Mapelli, and Arcara (2016, Carocci Edition), whose ideas are here further developed and extended.

1 Principles, objectives and settings

This chapter illustrates the main features of the methodology used in clinical neuropsychology. It first defines the core principles of the Interpretative Approach to the neuropsychological assessment. This is followed by an outline of this assessment, usually aiming to either provide a diagnosis that can complement a medical one, to define a cognitive profile of an examinee, or to design a rehabilitative intervention. Finally, the chapter describes the different types of neuropsychological settings that can be adopted for an assessment, outlining the role of the neuropsychologist and their relationship with the examinee.

1.1 Rationale of this book: an Interpretative Approach to neuropsychological assessment

Clinical neuropsychology has a decades-long tradition in many countries and has witnessed an increased interest on a global scale, as clearly demonstrated by the many available clinical neuropsychological tools that are developed for any linguistic or cultural context (Pedraza & Mungas, 2008). However, this growing interest over the years has not been accompanied by an increased interest in developing a shared and explicit methodological approach. Indeed, the methodology of the assessment is hardly the focus of most textbooks, and key aspects such as the interpretation of the results are often neglected or only briefly explained (Casaletto & Heaton, 2017).

There have been many approaches proposed during the history of neuropsychology (Russell, 2011; Goldstein & Incagnoli, 1997), often well-developed and based on clear rationales and foundations. However, these approaches have not been widely applied and mostly focused on the contexts in which they were originally developed, and for this reason, they have been less and less cited in clinical neuropsychological literature.

DOI: 10.4324/9781003195221-1

The current practice of neuropsychological assessment often lacks a clear rationale on how to carry out an evaluation in specific circumstances. For instance, a common question that may arise during clinical practice is "May I use a psychometric test if an examinee's feature (e.g., age) is not included in the normative data of that test?" or "May I perform a neuropsychological assessment without any neuropsychological tests?" or "If the examinee interrupts a test with several questions, how can I interpret their final scores in that test?" These and many other questions are very common in standard practice, but hardly covered in neuropsychology textbooks and often left to the clinician's expertise and point of view, developed over the years of practice. Given the lack of precise shared methodological foundations, there are currently many different ways to practice clinical work, with nuances that may affect the conclusions drawn during and after the assessment.

Another key aspect often neglected in traditional neuropsychological literature concerns the role of the neuropsychologist. Throughout this book, we will explain the relevance of the neuropsychologist in several aspects of the neuropsychological assessment, from selecting the appropriate setting (section 1.3) and psychometric tests, to administering them and interpreting the results in a comprehensive manner. Critically, the neuropsychologist should integrate and *interpret* all the available information (demographic and anamnestic information, the outcome of the psychometric assessment, and other qualitative observations) to provide a neuropsychological diagnosis, a description of the prognosis and suggestions for possible interventions.

In the present book, therefore, we aim to provide a framework for neuropsychological assessment, which we call an Interpretative Approach to the neuropsychological assessment. Based on three possible neuropsychological settings (see section 1.3), we specifically focus on the role of the neuropsychologist in the process of assessment and on the methodology used to reach a neuropsychological diagnosis. Hence this offers a clear guide to evaluate possible deficits following impairments of neurological nature or other. No clinical pathologies, syndromes or specific cognitive functions are considered and no specific neuropsychological tests are described and suggested.

The Interpretative Approach proposed in this book is based on the following key principles:

1 *The neuropsychologist plays an active role in every aspect of the neuropsychological assessment.* A common misconception in clinical neuropsychology (or in clinical processes in general) is to consider the

clinician as a passive collector of evidence, whose active role is limited to the formulation of a diagnosis. This is inaccurate for many reasons. First, the evidence collected during the neuropsychological assessment is always actively influenced by the neuropsychologist. This means interpreting a specific behaviour (like a linguistic error as evidence of a paraphasia) rather than simply reporting it, or understanding the reasons underlying the absence of expected behaviour (for example the lack of complaints of memory impairment following a brain injury). The neuropsychologist's knowledge and their constant analysis and interpretation of the examinee's behaviour, therefore play a crucial role in the outcome of the neuropsychological assessment. Throughout the book we will underline this active role as a crucial part of the neuropsychological assessment, from the initial interview to the test scoring, interpretation and the neuropsychological diagnosis.

2 *The neuropsychological assessment is a rational process of collecting evidence on the cognitive status of an examinee and of drawing a conclusion.* Key evidence is provided by the results on the neuropsychological tests, in addition to other sources, such as the anamnesis and the qualitative observations during tests' performance.

This leads to a third principle:

3 *In any neuropsychological assessment, the neuropsychologist must integrate and interpret all the available evidence to draw a conclusion.* This implies that neuropsychological tests alone are not sufficient to draw firm conclusions on any cognitive process or its impairment, in line with Lezak (2012). In the present book, we will illustrate this point by discussing neuropsychological cases in which integrating information and reasoning on them is crucial for a meaningful interpretation of test scores leading to a correct neuropsychological diagnosis (Chapter 8 and 9).

The importance of taking into account all the available evidence illustrates why self-administered neuropsychological assessments are only feasible in some specific cases, for instance to monitor the recovery of cognitive functions, and should be considered with extreme caution.

Given the relevance of tests in the neuropsychological assessment, a core principle of this approach is specifically about the use of test results.

4 *The use of results from neuropsychological tests always implies an active interpretation made by the neuropsychologist.* This principle is centred on the recognition of an active role of the neuropsychologist

when interpreting test results to reach a diagnosis. This challenges the more common belief that neuropsychological tests alone are informative of the cognitive status of an examinee, and instead always require an interpretation or inference made by the neuropsychologist. This concept is widely explained in par 4.3 and in par 6.2 of the textbook.

A fifth important point at the core of the Interpretative Approach (strictly related to the previous ones) is the following:

5   *The neuropsychologist should be aware of implicit inferences when interpreting available evidence.* A common bias during the neuropsychological assessment is to ignore the implicit inferences that are made during the diagnostic process. For instance, (and related to assumption 4), a neuropsychologist who administers a short-term memory test, may implicitly assume that the score actually provides information about an examinee's short term memory. However, there are many inferences beyond this apparently simple interpretation. For illustrative examples: i) the neuropsychologist assumes that the examinee was motivated enough to perform the task in a proper way (see par 4.3, and Chapter 6); ii) when using normative data to interpret an examinee's performance, the neuropsychologist implicitly assumes that they are adequate for a comparison (see Chapter 6); iii) If an impaired result is interpreted as evidencing a memory deficit, it is assumed that other potential deficits (e.g., an attentional one) did not play a relevant role.

There are many implicit inferences that are constantly made during the neuropsychological assessment, some particularly important to be taken into account. Identifying these inferences (either implicit or not) requires an *active* role of the neuropsychologist as part of the overall assessment.

Finally, a sixth principle is the following:

6   *A 'neuropsychological assessment' can be considered as such, only if there has been a direct observation of the examinees' behaviour and a direct interaction with them.* This principle implies that the most recent options of self-administration of neuropsychological tests (see setting C, section 1.3.3) cannot be considered a full assessment. This principle implies also that the administration of tests by an assistent, followed by an interpretation of a neuropsychologist who only analyzes the

test scores cannot be considered an actual neuropsychological assessment, unless it is also accompanied by a direct (in-person or remote) assessment of the examinee by the neuropsychologist (see Russel, 2011, for a discussion).

★★★★

The methodology described in this book illustrates how these principles may help understanding several issues a neuropsychologist faces when performing a neuropsychological assessment. Altogether, these principles may be considered the basis of the Interpretative Approach to the neuropsychological assessment.

1.2 Objectives of a neuropsychological assessment

The general aim of the neuropsychological assessment is to define the cognitive and behavioural status of an examinee in terms of cognitive mechanisms preserved and/or impaired (Lezak et al., 2012).

The assessment of an examinee's cognitive and behavioural profile is essential in a number of circumstances, for example:

1 When contributing to the medical diagnosis of an examinee, whenever the cognitive status is specifically associated with an illness, or when it may inform on the prognosis of an illness.
2 To distinguish between partially overlapping pathologies, for instance between a depressive pseudodementia and a dementia, or between depression and inertia following a frontal lobe lesion.
3 To evaluate an examinee's independence in daily activities.
4 To define a rehabilitation programme.
5 To certify the cognitive status for legal or insurance-related purposes, such as following an accident or when deciding if an examinee is suitable for driving or managing an electric wheelchair or to establish their suitability for a job.

Let's look at each of these circumstances in detail.

1.2.1 Contribution to medical diagnosis

The outcome of the neuropsychological assessment can contribute to or even anticipate the medical diagnosis of some pathologies. This is because in many cases, the cognitive status may be indicative of an underlying pathology (e.g., Feinkohl et al., 2019). For instance, dementia clearly illustrates how a neuropsychological assessment may reveal prodromic signs even when an individual is still fully independent and therefore dementia-related signs are not yet evident from a medical perspective (Mortamais et al., 2017).

In other cases, the neuropsychological assessment aims to provide prognostic information on some medical conditions, in particular those that have no specific neurological correlates and yet have an impact on the nervous system. For instance, heart-related or respiratory diseases, or diabetes, impact on the central nervous system because they indirectly affect brain metabolism and therefore impact on cognition (e.g., Zilliox et al., 2016). This is because the brain has a high level of metabolic requirements, which imply the correct functioning of a number of organs. As another example, a kidney disorder may result in neurotoxicity due to excess of uremic-acid which in turn impacts at the cognitive level; in another case, hyperammonemia produced by the liver may result in hepatic encephalopathy symptoms (Assem et al., 2018).

These examples illustrate how cognitive deficits are indeed common in medical practice, although they are not always detected, therefore emphasising the importance of complementing a medical diagnosis with a neuropsychological assessment.

1.2.2 Distinction between partially overlapping pathologies

The neuropsychological assessment allows us to disambiguate between pathologies such as a depressive pseudodementia -which is characterised by a prevalence of depressive symptoms- and clinical dementia (Kang et al., 2014). A depressive state is often characterised by memory and attention-related deficits that resemble those found at the initial stages of dementia (Perini et al., 2019).

On the other hand, mood disorders, including a tendency towards depressive symptoms, can characterise Alzheimer's disease due to an examinee's awareness of their own decline (Azocar, Livingston, & Huntley, 2021). For instance, it is important to detect fluctuations of cognitive performance within a neuropsychological assessment (expected in an examinee with depression) and to identify other qualitative aspects of an examinee's performance which may contribute to exclude a diagnosis of clinical dementia (Formánek, Csajbók, Wolfová, et al. 2020). A person with dementia, differently from pseudodementia, is typically characterised by lack of awareness of their own cognitive performance, and a focus on feelings of solitude and dissatisfaction (Sun et al., 2021).

Another case that illustrates the importance of a correct neuropsychological diagnosis is when two pathologies have similar symptoms but distinct origins. For instance, depression is typically accompanied by low voice and energy level, flat expression and motor slowness (Buyukdura, McClintock, & Croarkin, 2011). These symptoms are similar to abulia, aedonia, inertia, and diminished initiative that are typically observed in examinees with prefrontal lesions (Cohen, 1999). The two pathologies share similar manifestations but have very different aetiologies: one psychiatric, the other neurological.

Hence, a critical role of a neuropsychological assessment is to identify the features and the underlying causes of these symptomatologies in order to appropriately distinguish between them and reach the correct diagnosis.

1.2.3 Assessment of an examinee's independence in day-to-day activities

The neuropsychological assessment may aim to provide the assessment of an individual's day-to-day difficulties and to evaluate their daily-living independence, rather than providing a mere list of impaired and spared cognitive functions. This means using information from the neuropsychological assessment to directly evaluate an examinee's ability to look after themselves independently, their suitability to attend school and to work, as well as to drive or to have caring responsibilities, This is especially important for an examinee and their family who need planning how to reorganise their life following a neurological event.

Some examinees may be functional in their daily-living despite poor performance in psychometric tests (or vice versa). Correlation between daily living activities and cognitive functioning in clinical samples, can indeed be moderate (Jefferson et al., 2006). This may be supported by the mere repetition of familiar actions and patterns rather than reflecting a high cognitive functioning. Thus a neuropsychological·assessment requires a careful and deeper analysis of an examinee's cognitive abilities to understand any discrepancy with other, more or less demanding daily living activities.

1.2.4 Planning a rehabilitative intervention

To plan a rehabilitative intervention, the neuropsychological assessment aims to provide a clear profile of the impaired and spared cognitive, emotional and behavioural features of an examinee. The goal of such an intervention is, typically, to facilitate the examinee's adjustment in their daily living following the cerebral damage, and therefore the treatment has to be tailored around their individual needs (Wade, 2020). The neuropsychological assessment needs to take into account the examinee's cognitive and behavioural style as well as their residual social competences and background knowledge.

Multiple cognitive impairments require an accurate evaluation of the priorities for the treatment. For example, in an aphasic examinee who is also acalculic, the language problem probably needs to be addressed first in order to facilitate the examinee's communication, followed by the treatment of the mathematical abilities (Wilson, 2008). The initial neuropsychological assessment should also assess the examinee's awareness of their difficulties and to boost their motivation to engage with a demanding rehabilitative intervention.

At the end of the rehabilitative intervention, a second neuropsychological assessment needs to evaluate any changes that the examinee may have implemented. In this case, the assessment should consider a number of important aspects such as:

a   the possibility to administer the critical neuropsychological tests for a second time (after the treatment) yet limiting practice effects, for example by using parallel versions of a task used at the start of the assessment and using thresholds for significant change (see section 5.7.1).

b   the generalizability of any improvements following the rehabilitation. This can be achieved by administering tests that share the improved ability (e.g., naming) but assess it in a different modality (e.g., auditory and visual) or context.

1.2.5 Certifying the cognitive status for legal or insurance-related reasons

A neuropsychological assessment can also be used for forensic purposes, often based on specialised tests; for example, to certify the cognitive status for legal or insurance-related reasons, such as following an accident or when deciding if an examinee is suitable for driving or managing an electric wheelchair or to establish their suitability for a job, or to manage their own finances or even to assess an individual's imputability (e.g., Larrabee, 2012). In these cases, it is particularly important to exclude that the examinee may be malingering, and simulating their symptoms. This possibility is not necessarily investigated in most neuropsychological assessments.

1.3 The neuropsychological setting

By 'neuropsychological setting' we refer to the physical environment in which a neuropsychological assessment takes place, and also to the relationship between a neuropsychologist and an examinee, which can influence the outcome of the assessment.

In this textbook, we will mainly refer to the neuropsychological assessment that implies the active role of a clinical neuropsychologist. However, additional approaches have been implemented, which have been recently boosted during the lockdown period due to the COVID pandemic (Bilder et al., 2020). These approaches are now becoming more routinely used in clinical practice to complement traditional in-person neuropsychological services. They offer the opportunity to monitor the neuropsychological performance of examinees who live far away from a clinic, or whose mobility is impaired and therefore are less able to attend in-person clinics.

All settings should promote a positive relationship between the examinee and the neuropsychologist, which is of paramount importance for the assessment. Most examinees facing a neuropsychological assessment feel worried or anxious and the role of the neuropsychologist is to make the examinee feel comfortable and reassured. When appropriate, this may include informing the examinee on the aim and the procedure of the assessment, including the estimated duration.

In this section, we also discuss a specific setting that includes a self-assessment with digital tests. Although this setting is related to the overall process of neuropsychological assessment, when alone, it is not sufficient to be considered as a proper neuropsychological assessment (see section 1.0).

Two main types of setting can be distinguished – a traditional in-person and a remote setting – each with specific tools for assessment. The remote setting may involve the neuropsychologist or not (in this last case, tests are self-administered). The characteristics of these settings are reported in Figure 1.1 and in Table 1.1.

1.3.1 Traditional in-person setting (Setting A)

This is the traditional setting where the neuropsychologist and the examinee are in the same room, usually seated at a table, facing each other. The neuropsychologist uses the clinical interview and the collection of clinical and medical information to complete the examinee's anamnesis and clinical history. The psychometric component includes paper-and-pencil or digital tests (with the use of a computer, tablet or other devices) involving the direct interaction with the psychologist administering the tests.

In these latter cases, the examiner and the examinee are on the same side of the table both facing the computer screen, and depending on the examinee's abilities, the neuropsychologist explains the use of a computer or a tablet for performing the digital tests.

1.3.1.1 Main features of the traditional in-person setting

The environment should avoid any possible source of distraction or interference for an examinee, including neutral objects such as pens, books or paper. The physical environment should look different from a surgery/medical environment even when the assessment takes place in a hospital. Therefore, objects such as a bed, syringes and medications should not be visible as they may generate anxiety in an examinee and may disorient and confuse them regarding the nature of the examination.

The first critical feature consists of defining the roles of those involved directly or indirectly in the assessment.

a   *The neuropsychologist*: They should clearly explain the aim of the examination and the use of 'tests' to assess cognitive abilities. The neuropsychologist should always maintain a leadership role, guide the conversation and the examination, and at the same time show respect and interest for the examinee and for what they say. Maintaining leadership is particularly important when an examinee confabulates or diverges too much from the topics relevant for the assessment, or when an examinee is particularly disinhibited or excessively charming.

b   *The examinee*: Although the neuropsychologist keeps the leading role, the assessment is examinee-centered, and the examinee is encouraged to have an active and engaged role, from the initial interview and throughout the execution of the tests.

c   *Other professionals*: These may be medical doctors or trainees who can directly or indirectly be involved in the examination. Their role is to provide information regarding the examinee's condition or behaviour, or to observe the assessment and offer their perspective.

d   *Carers/Significant others*: Those who look after the examinee, typically family members or external caregivers. Their role is to provide additional and complementing information regarding the behaviour of the examinee in the home environment and any information that may contribute to the diagnosis.

It is important to note that the ideal setting of a neuropsychological assessment may often result in an 'artificial' environment because a relatively small, well-presented and well-articulated amount of information is presented to an examinee. This, however, is likely to be very different from the more complex and fast-paced environment an examinee lives in, therefore increasing the chance that a neuropsychological investigation may miss out or underestimate the severity of some cognitive problems.

1.3.2 Remote setting with neuropsychologist (Setting B)

A recent change in neuropsychological practice for assessment purposes consists of interacting with examinees online either with video or phone calls (i.e., teleneuropsychology, see Bilder, 2020; Zanin et al., 2022). This may also extend to discussing the performance of computer-based tasks that examinees have been instructed to perform independently. This setting provides a more ecological perspective for the examinee, although less controlled for the neuropsychological assessment.

The above rules defining the interaction between a neuropsychologist and an examinee are all still relevant in distance settings, and even more so when the interaction is purely verbal, i.e., on the phone, because it is more difficult to capture mood or other changes, which may affect the assessment.

Remote settings can take two main formats: via phone or video call, using adapted or newly created tests, in addition to a neuropsychological interview.

The setting here is completely different from the previous one. The examinee typically is in their own home on the phone or in front of a computer. In the case of a telephone call, the interaction is only verbal, while in the case of a video call the neuropsychologist and the examinee can see each other remotely, although the context in which the assessment takes place is only partially controlled.

The aim of an examination based on setting B is to test for any changes following a previous diagnosis received by an examinee, or to substitute the traditional in-person neuropsychological assessment if this is not feasible. For instance, this may be the case of an examinee with an event involving brain damage, initially resulting in some cognitive impairment, and subsequently improving. In such cases, the remote examination aims to establish that the cognitive improvement is maintained long-term, or to signal any changes (see Chapter 9).

Testing by phone requires questions with verbal answers. It is also possible to use an imagery task referring to common, well-known objects (e.g., a clock) to test visuospatial information processing mediated by a verbal answer. In the case of a video call, it is also possible to show a limited set of visual stimuli and ask to process them, for instance to name or to describe them, as long as the answer is verbal.

A neuropsychologist directly interviews, observes, and tests the examinee and can adapt or change questions if necessary. Since there is no in-person interaction in this setting, it is particularly important to be able to facilitate the interaction with the examinee and encourage their participation. A neuropsychologist therefore needs to pay particular attention to pragmatic elements of conversation, such as taking turns, waiting appropriately for an answer, as well as control their own voice and rhythm of speaking. For further suggestions see Bilder et al., 2020.

1.3.3 Remote setting with self-administered psychometric tests (Setting C)

This setting consists of a computer-based neuropsychological assessment with self-administration of the test, whereby the instructions are read and understood by the examinee (Feenstra et al., 2018). The aim of an examination based on setting C is to monitor cognitive performance in examinees with well-preserved cognitive skills but with special needs, for example individuals at risk of changes, such as age-related decline. In line with one of the principles of our approach, it follows that data

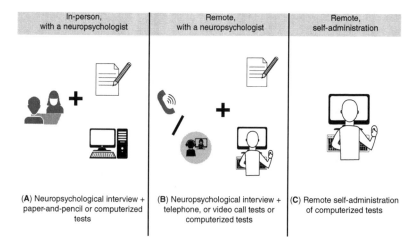

Figure 1.1 The three main settings related to the neuropsychological assessment. Setting A is *in-person*, setting B is *remote*, setting C is *remote with self-administered tests*.

Table 1.1 Specific features of Settings A, B, C

Type of setting	Label	Tools	Aim of the assessment	Role of the neuropsychologist
Traditional in-person setting	A	Interview + Paper-and-pencil tests + digital tests	Initial diagnostic or in depth diagnostic	In-person interaction to assess the examinee's cognitive abilities and behaviour
Remote setting with the neuropsychologist	B	Phone call or video call + tests adapted to be used in call + interview	Follow-up after an in-person assessment of a pathology. Initial diagnostic or in depth diagnostic if in-person diagnostic is not possible	Remote interaction to test for any changes following an initial diagnosis
Remote setting without the neuropsychologist	C	Self-administered on-line psychometric tests	Monitoring the evolution of cognitive performance mostly in absence of a pathology, e.g., in healthy ageing or following the full recovery from an illness	Limited to the selection of the on-line psychometric tests and the analysis of the results with no contact with the examinee

collection from this setting alone cannot be considered a 'neuropsy-chological assessment' because it lacks the direct interaction with the examinee and the observations made by the neuropsychologist during the assessment.

Performance is recorded, and depending on the testing plan, results may be sent to the neuropsychologist. In some cases, only a pre-recorded human voice encourages the examinee to continue testing by giv-ing comments or reinforcements. This setting cannot be controlled by the neuropsychologist in the same way as in the traditional neu-ropsychological assessment. Indeed there is no direct interaction and the neuropsychologist cannot collect and interpret information about the examinee's attitude towards testing and their verbal and non-verbal behaviour during testing (e.g., whether they are distracted, nervous or anxious) which is essential for the diagnosis.

Since there is no neuropsychologist present, no information regard-ing prosody and body language can be collected, and no relationship as such is established. This information however, is typically collected in previous in-person meetings with the examinee, and the self-administered testing is typically a follow up for recovering examinees or those who may be at risk of developing progressive cognitive decline and therefore need to be regularly assessed.

Therefore, examinees suitable for testing in setting C are typically fully independent and able to understand task instructions.

Setting C may also be useful for neuropsychological research or for rehabilitation purposes as it allows regular testing and monitor-ing of cognitive changes at distance. The present textbook will pro-vide limited information on this specific setting, since there is no yet sufficient data to evaluate its impact and robustness in clinical neuropsychology.

1.4 The timeline and the main tools of the neuropsychological assessment

In settings A (in-person) and B (remote with neuropsychologist), the neuropsychological assessment can be defined by three main temporal steps (see Figure 1.2): before meeting the examinee, during the meet-ing and after the meeting. These represent common standards, but depending on many aspects (e.g., available time, whether is a first visit or a follow-up) the steps may change. During these steps, information regarding the examinee's mental, physical and cognitive status should be obtained by previously collected information, as well as directly by interviewing and assessing the examinee. Collectively, this information

Timeline	Neuropsychological assessment phase	Chapter
Before meeting the examinee	Anamnesis	2–3
During the meeting with the examinee	Anamnesis Interview Psychometric tests Preliminary diagnosis Feedback	2–3–4–6–7
After meeting the examinee	Diagnostic reasoning Diagnosis Report	8

Figure 1.2 Main features of the neuropsychological assessment along a timeline (before meeting the examinee, during the meeting with the examinee and after the meeting), and corresponding chapters where these features are discussed.

gathered during the examination allows the neuropsychologist to formulate a final neuropsychological diagnosis, which should be communicated to the examinee and their family via an initial feedback and more formally in a report.

2 Anamnesis and semeiotics

This chapter discusses the two important concepts of *anamnesis* and *semeiotics* in the neuropsychological assessment. In particular, the anamnesis is based on information coming from the examinee's medical, psychological and cognitive history, whereas neuropsychological semeiotics incorporates information provided by behavioural and cognitive signs and symptoms, gathered throughout the assessment. This chapter follows the timeline outlined in Chapter 1 (Figure 1.2).

2.1 Before meeting the examinee: anamnestic information about the examinee (neuropsychological anamnesis)

The anamnesis is a fundamental component of a neuropsychological assessment and diagnosis (Lezak et al., 2012). Anamnestic information should be collected prior to the neuropsychological assessment itself; for example, by reading reports of past neuropsychological assessments the examinee underwent. This information is important to guide the interpretation of the examinee's cognitive, emotional and behavioural profile. The close relationship between emotional and cognitive processing makes knowledge of the examinee's psychological history essential (Pimental, O'Hara, & Jandak, 2018). As well as being collected prior to the psychometric assessment, this information is further corroborated and integrated during the neuropsychological interview.

A neuropsychological anamnesis should include any data or information that allows establishing a possible link between the observed cognitive deficits following an illness of organic, medical or psychological origin. Relevant information can be collected through the initial neuropsychological interview, from any past examinations available and from medical reports. Additional data can also be collected by questionnaires such as the Cognitive Reserve Index

DOI: 10.4324/9781003195221-2

questionnaire (Nucci et al., 2011; see Appendix 2). For further details on the neuropsychological anamnesis and its contribution to the diagnostic reasoning see also Chapter 8 and Table 8.1.

The anamnesis should cover three main aspects, the Medical, Psychological and Cognitive history of the examinee.

2.1.1 Medical history

This includes any health-related issues throughout an examinee's life, which helps to define a neuropsychological diagnosis. Besides interviewing the examinee, their medical history can be reconstructed by reading the medical records when the examinee is admitted, or the reports of any past medical examinations. The relevant medical information should be selected prior to the meeting with an examinee, and further information can also be obtained from the examinees themselves.

From the medical history the following information should be collected:

a   *Neuro-imaging scans*: These can include Computerised Axial Tomography – CT, Magnetic Resonance Imaging – MRI, Electroencephalogram – EEG, Positron Emission Tomography – PET, Single Photon Emission Tomography – SPECT, receptor examinations (e.g., receptor SPECT).

b   *Medications*: This is an important source of information about an examinee's health, as they can easily be traced back to any current or past disease.

c   *Other medical examinations*: Including the results of blood tests that could indicate the presence of metabolic deficits (vitamin B12 or folate deficiency) potentially causing reversible cognitive disorders (e.g., Kouvari et al., 2022), the presence of internal pathologies such as diabetes or hepatic encephalopathy, or the presence of cardiovascular pathologies (e.g., López-Franco et al., 2021).

d   *Sensory deficits in hearing or visual acuity*: These should be ascertained prior to the neuropsychological assessment since they determine the choice and exclusion of the cognitive tests to be used. For instance, during the interview and anamnestic collection, the presence of hearing deficits that prevent a clear perception of the questions asked should be noted.

e   *Biological rhythms*: Information about sleep-wake or hunger-satiety may signal the presence of hypothalamic or other organic alterations or linked to psychiatric pathologies such as anxiety and depression. For instance, this can be signalled by frequent sleep interruptions or difficulties in falling asleep (e.g., Murphy & Peterson, 2015).

f   *Information with no apparent causal link with an examinee's current cognitive deficits*: This may include knowledge about any surgery, hospital admissions, medications and any past or present pathologies. This may also comprise pathologies that do not have a direct link with cognition, such as diabetes, or metabolic disorders, which could nevertheless affect cognitive abilities (Feinkohl et al., 2019) sometimes in a reversible way (Zilliox et al., 2016). It is also important to collect information about episodes that might appear unrelated to a cognitive disorder itself, but that may nevertheless be a trigger for them. For instance, this is the case of breaking a bone in an ageing adult which may reduce their physical and subsequently cognitive independence, and possibly accelerate an underlying degenerative pathology.

2.1.2 Psychological history

Psychological history concerns the collection and description of all significant episodes of the examinee's recent and past life. Some events are undoubtedly of significant impact (e.g., death of spouse or child, business failure, losing a job, separation/divorce), others may have a more subjective relevance within an individual's life and value-system (e.g., the death of a pet or retirement) (e.g., Luhmann et al., 2012). In these cases, the initial interview can only highlight an examinee's emotional participation in these events, which should be acknowledged by the neuropsychologist. These events within an examinee's history may trigger strong emotional reactions and mood changes, and also cause cognitive alterations such as attention or memory deficits in absence of brain lesions. In some cases, these episodes may also have medical implications because they may result in admission to psychiatric units for disorders such as panic attacks or depression.

The psychological history should also include information regarding the social and emotional relationships surrounding the examinee, which describe the examinee's support network and indirectly their ability to interact with others, and their psychological well-being. This may also offer insights into the family's dynamics, including any tensions which may induce affective-emotional disorders resulting in behavioural problems and transitory cognitive disorders which may be explained by underlying stress.

At times, prolonged stressful and wearing situations lead to chronic stress which impacts on cognitive abilities because of the important physiological and hormonal changes that accompany it (see Chapter 9).

2.1.3 Cognitive history

Cognitive history refers to the knowledge and the abilities that an examinee has acquired throughout their life, and that modulates their brain and cognitive functioning (in Lezak et al. 2012 this is mentioned as *social history*).

Cognitive history has long been limited to counting the years of education or the education level achieved by an examinee (elementary, diploma, degree or higher), but it is now clear that an examinee's education is only one of the many factors that needs to be taken into account when evaluating their cognitive history. Indeed, an examinee's cognitive abilities may be influenced by many other cultural, social and physical experiences as well as the environment where they lived. For instance, whether they studied or worked abroad, whether they are bilingual, or whether they played a musical instrument, whether they cultivated any hobbies or special interests, or actively participated in the social or political life of their community.

The examinee's cognitive history signalling the degree of competence achieved as well as the richness and the continuity of mental engagement in social, cultural and leisure activities can be referred to as "Cognitive Reserve" (Stern, 2009). This concept has initially been used in relation to the onset of the clinical symptoms of dementia (Katzman et al., 1988), such as the manifestation of these symptoms may be delayed by the examinee's cognitive reserve. The concept of Cognitive Reserve has now been extended to other non-degenerative pathologies and healthy ageing (e.g., Menardi et al., 2019; Steward et al., 2018; Rosenich et al., 2020).

In the context of healthy ageing, cognitive reserve has mainly been indexed by formal education (e.g., Rosselli et al, 2009), or by other proxies of premorbid intelligence using tests such as the NART (Nelson, 1982; Garrett et al, 2010).

More recently, cognitive reserve and premorbid cognitive state have also been estimated taking into account other indexes (Meng & D'Arcy, 2012), such as an examinee's working activity (Pool et al., 2016) and leisure activities (Fratiglioni et al., 2004) which may involve different cognitive skills, commitments and responsibilities all contributing to increase an examinee's cognitive reserve. Because of the variability in measuring these activities, studies considering the concept of cognitive reserve often estimate it in a heterogeneous manner (Meng & D'Arcy, 2012).

2.2 Meeting the examinee: information gathered directly from the examinee (neuropsychological semeiotics)

Neuropsychological semeiotics concerns the collection of the examinee's signs and symptoms to formulate a neuropsychological diagnosis. This begins with the neuropsychological interview (see Chapter 3) and then proceeds with the administration of formal tests.

A symptom is a manifestation of a pathological condition that is experienced by the examinee themselves (e.g., feeling dizzy, or reporting forgetfulness), while a sign is a manifestation of a pathological condition perceived by the neuropsychologist (e.g., disartria, disinhibition, etc.). The difference between symptoms and signs lies in their degree of subjectivity: *symptoms* are subjectively identified and referred to by an examinee, whereas *signs* are detected and reported by a clinician or a neuropsychologist by observing an examinee's behaviour, speech, and posture both during the interview and during the administration of the tests.[1] Signs can also be recognised by detecting behaviours that occur between one test and another or when the examinee enters or leaves the assessment room.

Symptoms can be directly collected from the examinee's narrative and from the interview with carers (see Table 2.1). Symptoms may either denote a loss of general well-being, such as asthenia, loss of appetite,

Table 2.1 Symptoms and signs

Symptoms	Signs
Reported during the neuropsychological interview	Observed by the neuropsychologist during the whole assessment or collected during the anamnesis
1 Reported by the examinee 2 Reported by a carer	1 During the anamnesis (e.g., sings described in a previous report or reported by a carer) 2 During the neuropsychological interview (anamnestic signs) 3 During the psychometric assessment (diagnostic signs) 4 When a diagnosis is formulated (prognostic signs)

rather than referring to a specific disease. An examinee may report a symptom, which may or may not be confirmed at neuropsychological assessment. For example, loss of memory can be subsequently confirmed with appropriate neuropsychological tests (keeping in mind that the examinee may also simulate the reported impairments).

Neuropsychological semeiotics complements medical semeiotics, which refers to the collection of information (signs and symptoms) during a medical examination. The neuropsychological diagnosis should take into account the conclusions of the medical diagnosis, when available. This is based on collecting clinical symptoms and signs in order to formulate a range of possibilities for the most likely diagnosis of a disease and differentiate between diseases that may share signs and symptoms.

2.2.1 How signs and symptoms can be detected

2.2.1.1 Stage 1: Neuropsychological interview

Signs: During the assessment, the neuropsychologist may become aware of signs (defined as *Anamnestic Signs*) when they first meet an examinee. These signs indicate the existence of past diseases or conditions that are relevant when assessing the current state of the examinee. For example, an examinee with a paretic limb suggests that they may have had a stroke.

During the interview, the neuropsychologist may also detect some signs from the examinee's behaviour, useful for the final diagnosis or to interpret other parts of the assessment (as the results of the test). The examinee, for example, may show anomias or semantic paraphasias, which the neuropsychologist may interpret as a sign of memory or language deficit.

Symptoms: An examinee may also provide useful information regarding symptoms for the diagnosis, for example they may report having memory problems. These problems – as well as changes in behaviour or mood – may also be confirmed or even reported in the first place by carers, for instance in case of examinees not fully aware of their own disorders.

2.2.1.2 Stage 2: Psychometric assessment

After the interview, an examinee is typically assessed with a set of appropriately selected neuropsychological tests. Thus, at this stage only signs can be detected, and crucially they are used for the recognition and identification of a disease and for the final diagnosis.

Signs: While performing psychometric tests, an examinee may show a variety of signs. For example, an examinee may perform well in a 'Figure Copy Test', but they may hold the pencil in such a way that is suggestive of a motor disorder in using tools (this may be a sign of apraxia, agnosia for the pencil or a superficial motor impairment). Performance in a psychometric test could be considered a sign according to the above definition, although typically the term sign in neuropsychology indicates qualitative aspects of behaviour which are relevant for the diagnosis.

2.2.2 Examples of the main signs typically associated with disorders of specific cognitive functions

Language disorders (production and comprehension):

- Mumbled or slurred language
- Monotone and flattened voice, total or partial loss of prosody
- Impoverished language with semantically and syntactically simplified structure
- Phonemic paraphrasias, semantic paraphrasias, conduites d'approche
- Anomias and/or circumlocutions;
- Echolalias
- Impaired comprehension or comprehension preserved only for simple orders
- Required repetition of questions and tasks instructions in absence of sensory problems such as deafness

Attention disorders:

- Distractibility from environmental stimuli
- Abrupt change of topic of conversation during the administration of tests;
- Several reminders to concentrate are required

Memory disorders:

- Struggle to remember even basic biographical data (e.g., phone number, house address or even their date of birth)
- Struggle to remember task instructions
- Tendency to repeat information
- Confabulations: the tendency to fill-in an examinee's own memory gaps by providing logically consistent answers, even if the contents are clearly implausible (also in the case of executive dysfunctions)

Orientation disorders:

• Struggle to orient themselves in space and time, even when prompts are provided

Visuo-spatial disorders:

• Failure to keep their gaze on target
• Imbalanced posture towards one side, sometimes observable when dressing up, for example, a jacket badly sleeved on, or glasses resting unbalanced over one ear

Executive functions disorders:

• Disinhibition, for example, if an examinee appears disrespectful, does not follow turns during the interview or the most basic social conventions, tends to speak on top of the neuropsychologist, at times with rude language
• Perseverations in language as well as in some movements
• Hyperactive and/or agitated behaviour
• Abulia, lack of any initiative including in communication, impoverished speech, tendency to respond 'only if questioned' with laconic and telegraphic answers. Flattened facial expressions, and monotone voice

Awareness disorders:

• Lack of concern or total indifference to own or others' emotional or clinical conditions

Throughout this textbook, we will see how the signs and symptoms of the examinee – collected during the neuropsychological interview with the examinee and family members – the anamnesis and the psychometric assessment, should all be integrated as important information that can help to interpret available evidence and reach a neuropsychological diagnosis.

2.3 At the end of the meeting: preliminary diagnosis and feedback to the examinee

Once the results of psychometric tests and other medical investigations are completed, the neuropsychologist may formulate a preliminary diagnosis unless the presence of Pathognomonic Signs indicates a particular disease beyond doubt (this is, however, very rare in both medical and neuropsychological fields). A preliminary neuropsychological diagnosis should be then communicated, highlighting the prognostic signs which indicate the possible development of an examinee's health and future life.

Neuropsychological semeiotics therefore requires both in-depth clinical knowledge and also logical and deductive skills to link the diagnostic elements and to correctly interpret all available evidence on an examinee. This is further discussed in Chapter 8.

Note

1. Note that the term 'symptoms' is often colloquially used to denote both subjective symptoms and objective signs, for example 'symptoms of dementia' could indicate an objective memory impairment. At times, this ambiguity can cause confusion.

3 The neuropsychological interview

This chapter discusses how to perform a clinical interview within the context of a neuropsychological assessment (see timeline, Figure 1.2). For settings implying a direct interaction with a neuropsychologist (A and B, see Chapter 2), the chapter provides advice on how to perform an interview collecting information about the examinee's verbal communication abilities, including their fluency and errors. For settings involving interactions with the neuropsychologist (A, B if via video call) advice on how to collect information on non-verbal communication abilities is also presented. For setting A, the chapter also provides guidance on how to perform an interview with an examinee's carer, in order to collect further evidence, since caregivers typically know examinees from a more ecological perspective.

For remote setting C, with self-administration, the interview is not carried out, and it is typically conducted in previous meetings with different settings (either A or B).

3.1 Theoretical features of the neuropsychological interview

The interview is often considered one of the most important tools in a neuropsychologist's profession, with a clear distinction between the neuropsychological setting and the psycho-diagnostic one (see also Hebben & Milberg, 2009; Abbate & Trimarchi, 2013). In neuropsychology, good communication skills and the ability to flexibly use the best interview techniques and strategies are essential professional tools. Flexibility is important because neuropsychological interviews typically follow a semi-structured outline in which some topics to be discussed with the examinee are planned ahead, although the conversation is always tailored around the examinee's history and abilities.

DOI: 10.4324/9781003195221-3

An open and forthcoming relationship with an examinee is critically important to obtain an initial impression of the examinee. This is based on an attentive observation of the examinee's behaviour, such as language and posture, which is critical for the diagnosis.

An effective communicative exchange is also critical in encouraging an examinee's cooperation, motivation and their focus during the whole examination. This is particularly important when an examinee may be uncooperative due to tiredness, nervousness, irritation, or lack of understanding of the reasons for the assessment. Therefore, intrinsic in the neuropsychological interview is the focus on the examinee's neurological and cognitive status, including any associated mental health issue.

3.1.1 Reformulating and mirroring techniques

A way to promote effective communication is by means of two fundamental techniques in which the neuropsychologist returns prior expressions to the examinee. First, *reformulating* refers to rewording the examinee's prior talk that entails linguistic transformation (in grammar and/or lexicon). Second, *mirroring* in which a neuropsychologist instead selects and repeats a key part of the examinee's speech. These techniques have been successfully used in other disciplines, such as in psychotherapy-related contexts (Knol et al, 2020; Ferrara, 1994) and in marketing (Peterson & Limbu, 2009).

Reformulating refers to the reproduction of a preceding verbal expression by the examinee that carries and reflects the neuropsychologist's understanding of that expression. As the content of these prior talks becomes transformed, the neuropsychologist not merely rephrases what has been said but also negotiates what is relevant to the current conversation. Reformulation serves multiple goals (Voutilainen & Peräkylä, 2014), such as providing a summary of the examinee's talk, focusing on or filtering out specific aspects of a narrative, or facilitating a more specific investigation. Reformulating therefore facilitates a change from either a too detailed and complex, or a fragmented and sparse examinee's narrative into a more coherent account. Reformulating also helps a neuropsychologist to check the understanding of an examinee's talk, as well as helping an examinee gain insight into their status and thinking.

The second way to return an examinee's talk is in the form of *mirroring*, or the neuropsychologist repeating key elements of prior talk that are particularly important or interesting (Ferrara, 1994). For example, a neuropsychologist may repeat a specific adjective or word used by an examinee (see examples in the text for more details). This mirroring allows a neuropsychologist to *tune-in* to the examinee in order to understand their mood and shows the neuropsychologist's attentiveness, and it also promotes further analyses of the repeated elements. Repetitions achieve a double goal as they have a retrospective action while they also prepare the ground for the following conversation. This is achieved by highlighting the focus of the suggested response which allows the neuropsychologist to receive more relevant information about and from the examinee. Repetition also helps the examinee to increase their awareness of what has been said (Ferrara, 1994).

In a neuropsychological context, a communicative exchange is a complex interweaving of verbal and non-verbal messages between a neuropsychologist and an examinee who interact on the basis of their shared knowledge. This is a crucial aspect of the interview, because it reflects a number of cognitive abilities that are needed when effectively communicating with another person. These abilities are, for example, clarity of thoughts and language, 'theory of mind' (the ability to take another person's perspective into account, Martín-Rodríguez et al., 2010; Poletti et al., 2012), and other basic communication skills, such as the ability to 'take turns' (e.g., Rousseau, Daveluy, & Kozlowski, 2010).

Lack of consistency between verbal and non-verbal communication in an examinee requires careful consideration by the neuropsychologist because it may signal discomfort or difficulties experienced by the examinee. These may emerge in terms of change of mood, of voice intonation and drooping of the gaze especially in the context of specific topics.

Identifying these difficulties and making an examinee feel supported and understood throughout the neuropsychological assessment increases the chance that the evaluation reflects the veridical cognitive functioning of the examinee. Listening to an examinee's needs is essential to establish an empathic relationship, and to appreciate cognitive impairments (Darksen, Bensing & Lagro-Janssen, 2013).

3.1.2 Goals of the neuropsychological interview

3.1.2.1 Collecting information on an examinee's spontaneous language

During the neuropsychological interview (see timeline in Figure 1.2), the neuropsychologist has the opportunity to detect important technical aspects of an examinee's spontaneous language in a communicative context. The observation of the examinee's language in an unstructured (or semi-structured) context such as the interview, allows us to highlight possible differences between comprehension in a spontaneous and informal setting as opposed to the more structured testing conditions. Informal conversations are typically facilitated by factors such as gestures, facial expressions, modulation of the examiner's voice which are inevitably reduced during a formal assessment (Mast, 2007).

The interview is also important in informing a neuropsychologist about cases where language is typically intact; for instance, in examinees with neglect or major disorders in attention, or in the case of some memory disorders. The information about preserved language abilities in an examinee allows a neuropsychologist to plan the use of tests that require understanding or producing verbal material, even in a complex format.

The analysis of language during the interview allows us to classify the examinee's speech as *fluent* or *not-fluent*, to analyse its content and the appropriate use of pragmatic conversational rules, such as the use of shared knowledge and of alternating roles. Furthermore, in the case of fluent but quantitatively reduced language, or content-free and uninformative speech, the neuropsychologist may need to check whether the examinee's answers are relevant to the questions, or whether they are vague or too general. In this case, the examinee may need to be continuously prompted to specify or detail their answers in order to clarify the message they want to convey. In case of these fluent examinees, a neuropsychologist may also need to assess whether they lose track of the conversation and proceed by associations of ideas, which requires refocusing on the main points of conversation (Begolo et al., 2019). The neuropsychologist also needs to assess whether an examinee is able to consider the neuropsychologist's point of view during the conversation; for example, whether they assume a neuropsychologist knows about people or episodes referred to in an examinee's conversation (Deleau, 2012).

As well as the content, the format of the language and the presence of any abnormalities during the interview should be noted. These can be syntactic errors which can affect an entire sentence, or instead refer to individual words, for instance in the form of *anomias, anomic latencies, circumlocutions, echolalias, phonemic and/or semantic paraphasias, conduites d'approche and neologisms*. Errors in articulation should also be noted in order to understand their nature, for instance whether they are paretic, such as dysarthria, or whether they reflect problems of motor programming, such as apraxia of language.

3.1.2.2 *Collecting information on an examinee's orientation*

Assessing an examinee's speech production and comprehension during the interview addresses other relevant purposes. One is to test the examinee's spatial and temporal awareness, another is to obtain preliminary data on their episodic memory capacity, for instance by testing their understanding of the environment they live in (Lezak et al., 2012). This can be assessed by testing an examinee's knowledge of the main news, or of the names of politicians, entertainers or athletes involved in current events.

3.1.2.3 *Collecting information on an examinee's prerequisites for the psychometric examination*

Another goal of the neuropsychological interview is to assess whether an examinee has the cognitive prerequisites necessary for the psychometric examination that may follow. For example, if the examinee presents major difficulties in language production, only tests requiring motor answers (e.g., pointing) should be administered, whereas in the case of difficulties in comprehension, only tests whose instructions are simple and intuitive should be chosen.

During the neuropsychological interview, it is useful to fill in a form to note all the features of language listed above, as well as the examinee's mood, appropriateness of posture, their awareness of any cognitive deficits, and their emotional reactivity to specific issues. A good neuropsychological interview should therefore provide, in a short time, useful information to select the psychometric tests to be administered (this is especially important if a flexible approach on test selection is used, see section 4.10), as well as to formulate a preliminary diagnostic hypothesis that can guide the assessment.

3.2 Practical features of the neuropsychological interview

A number of strategies help the neuropsychologist to establish a relationship with an examinee. These may depend on the context and need to be used flexibly. These consist of a set of actions that may help the neuropsychologists and their relationship with the examinee. Importantly all these potential strategies should not be applied blindly by the neuropsychologist, but always pondered, and used depending on the context. For example, if the examinee seems anxious and shows signs of cognitive decline, the neuropsychologist may need to simplify the conversation. On the other hand, an examinee who is at ease and speaks fluently, may perceive questions that are too simple or a conversation that is too simplified as patronising.

1 *Ice-breaking*: Of key importance are the strategies that a neuropsychologist can use to open the interview. For settings A and B a typical start consists of asking the examinee predictable or *closed questions* for example related to their identity (such as: "What is your name?", "Where do you live?", "When were you born?"). Since the examinee is likely to answer these questions smoothly, the conversation can start easily, avoiding anxiety-provoking questions and demanding cognitive processing. Close questions are especially useful in this initial phase of the interview in order to reduce anxiety especially in fearful, worried or even frightened examinees, as well as to gather basic personal information on an examinee.

   Another type of simple opening, again for settings A and B are *two-forced choice questions* which aim to facilitate the examinee's response and thus encourage verbal production. For instance, instead of asking the question: "What do you do during the day?" it may be better to say: "Do you usually stay in or go out during the day?", or "Do you watch television? Do you read newspapers?". The choice should be among no more than two alternatives, and the questions should be short and clearly expressed so that the answer is not influenced by memory difficulties or language deficits.

   For setting C, which is fully remote with no direct contact with a neuropsychologist, it is still very important to engage with the examinee, and make them feel at ease with the assessment. Even if this assessment is fully self-administered, the examinee should be welcomed and guided through the evaluation via a recording of a human voice, possibly addressing them personally. Information about the examinee's well being, for instance whether they feel anxious or tired should also be collected using simple questions ("How are you today?", or "Do you feel anxious?", "Did you sleep well?") with graded answers.

2 *Open questions*: In the second phase of the neuropsychological interview in settings A and B, *open questions* can be gradually introduced. Different from close and two-forced questions, open ones do not have predictable answers and allow an examinee to speak freely and independently. These questions offer the neuropsychologist an opportunity to analyse an examinee's spontaneous speech especially in terms of how the content of the conversation is organised and delivered (e.g., presence of anomias, paraphasias, latencies, circumlocutions). Information on paraverbal and non-verbal components (see section 3.1.1) is also collected. In some cases the use of open questions needs to be closely monitored by the neuropsychologist, for instance if an examinee tends to digress on the

requested topic and thus needs to be brought back to the initial question. Any digressions or loss of the thread of the discourse should always be noted because it may signal disorders of working memory or executive functions.

No open questions can be asked in setting C.

3 *Prosody and language*: Both in the case of closed and open questions, a neuropsychologist should use verbal and non-verbal behaviour to engage with an examinee and encourage them to communicate. For instance, in settings A and B this may occur using appropriate posture, gestures and tone of voice, and showing expressions of surprise, interest, approval or disapproval in order to encourage exchange with the examinee. Expressions such as: "Tell me", "Yes, of course", "I understand", "Ah, interesting", "Can you think of anything else?" all encourage a positive interaction.

Throughout the interaction, the neuropsychologist should use a calm and clear voice, and always address the examinee directly and maintain good eye contact. The language should mirror the social and cultural background of the examinee, with everyday examples that are relevant for them (see mirroring technique, Knol et al, 2020; section 3.1.1).

Prosody and language, and in particular the use of the voice, are particularly important in setting B when the assessment occurs remotely. This is to make sure that an examinee is engaged and encouraged throughout the assessment. Prosody and language are also important for a neuropsychologist to understand an examinee's state of mind (for instance if their voice is trembling) and engagement (for instance if their voice is hesitant).

Prosody and language cannot be assessed in setting C.

4 *Body language*: In in-person settings (A), a neuropsychologist should accompany their verbal communication with the appropriate gesturing to facilitate comprehension. Yet unnecessary gesticulation should be avoided since it may interfere with the examinee's attention and distract them from the tests. Body language is only minimally involved in setting B (only if based on video call), and not in setting C.

5 *Tasks' instructions*: These need to be conveyed in a clear way, avoiding flat or inexpressive tone, and ensuring that they have been properly understood by an examinee, for instance by using practice questions. The neuropsychologist should avoid overloading the examinee with too much information in order to avoid confusion. The same indications should be followed in setting C using a recording of the instructions.

6 *Neuropsychologists' empathetic behaviour:* This is fundamentally important throughout the assessment and especially at the beginning of
a neuropsychologist-examinee relationship. Acknowledging the
examinee's wellbeing at this point in time can be assessed by asking simple questions such as "How do you feel right now?", "Do
you feel confused?", "Are you worried?". This will help the examinee feel that their emotions and challenges are important to the
neuropsychologist. In setting C, such questions can be asked using
a likert-scale questionnaire (see point 1, ice-breaking). Making an
examinee feel understood will facilitate the communication which
in turn will help a neuropsychologist to evaluate the examinee's
awareness of their impairments and the importance attributed to
them.

Empathy should also be demonstrated throughout the assessment
with verbal (settings A, and B) or written messages (setting C). For
instance, the neuropsychologist should encourage the examinee to
perform at their best, even when the tasks are challenging, especially
in examinees who have a tendency to lack confidence in their abilities and may give up the assessment. Yet, neuropsychologists should
avoid too much interference with an examinee's performance, or
give them the impression that they made too many errors.

3.3 Examples of a communicative exchange during interview

Here are some examples of dialogues between a neuropsychologist
(NPS) and an examinee (E) at the beginning of the neuropsychological interview in settings A and B. Information on prosody and body
language – where present – is provided in *italics* and parentheses at the
start of each exchange.

3.3.1 Example 1. Introducing the idea of a neuropsychological assessment (using Setting A)

In all examinations, examinees have to be clearly *introduced to the idea
of a neuropsychological assessment which requires full cooperation.* For example, in approaching an elderly examinee who is assessed for a suspected
dementia, a possible opening could be:

NPS: [*Smiling, keeping good eye contact and standing by the door to welcome the
examinee to come in and sit down*] Good morning Mrs. Smith. Can I
call you Mary? How are you today?

E: I am good, thank you.

NPS: [*Sounding clear and looking directly at the examinee, keeping arms unfolded and sitting straight*] I am doctor Mondini and today we are going to have a look at how your mind works, for example at your memory, language and concentration. Does this sound ok?

E: Yes, sure!

Or:

NPS: [*With a clear and welcoming voice*] How have you been feeling lately? Have you been feeling confused at times?

E: Well, yes … I occasionally feel a bit muddled.

NPS: [*Looking attentive at the examinee's words, and mirroring their words to indicate empathy and good understanding*] I understand, how often do you feel muddled?

E: Only occasionally.

NPS: [*Sounding keen and with an encouraging voice, and avoiding gesticulation*] Do you sometimes find it hard to remember the name of people or objects? OR Do you sometimes forget where you put some objects, for example your keys or glasses?

E: Yes, sometimes I do.

NPS: [*With a clear voice, after leaving a short pause*] Today, I will first ask you some facts about your life, and then I will ask you to perform some tests. Have you done any of these before?

E: Yes, I did!

NPS: [*Sounding sympathetic*] Oh good!

Good is a comment provided at the end of a short conversation to acknowledge something. For instance:

NPS: Have you ever done any tests before?

E: No!

NPS: [*With a reassuring voice*] Good, it will be something new! A bit like a game, although not completely the same.

3.3.2 Example 2. Introducing the idea of a neuropsychological assessment for an examinee who suffered a brain injury and needs to be cognitively assessed (using Setting A)

NPS: Good morning Richard, how are you doing today?

E: Very well, thank you.

NPS: [*With a clear and firm voice*] Do you know why you are here today?

E: "I am not so sure..."

NPS: It is because after your brain injury, there may still be some residual problems with your memory and with processing information
and therefore we need to examine them in detail. It's very important that you mention any difficulties you may have so we better
understand the situation.

Other more specific cases may be more challenging because the clinical
conditions of an examinee or their attitude make it difficult for them to
understand and be involved in the examination. These cases therefore
require a more flexible approach of the neuropsychologist to engage
with them. The examples below refer to an uncooperative examinee
and to one with a depressive mood. These examples also offer the
opportunity to find out how an assessment is introduced in the context
of setting B.

3.3.3 Example 3. Persuading a reluctant and uncooperative examinee (using Setting A)

E: [*Looking down, avoiding eye contact and fidgeting nervously with fingers and
holding his phone*] I didn't want to come here, I don't understand
what I'm doing here again to repeat the same trivial tests, as I have
so many other things to do.

NPS: [*Keeping a friendly look, maintaining eye contact and talking with an
encouraging voice*] You are right, it is never pleasant to do things you
don't want to do, and under the insistence of others. But why do
you think your son brought you here?

E: [*Sounding indignant, sitting straight and tense and barely waiting for their
turn to speak*] Because he keeps saying that I forget things, but it's
not true. At home I'm able to do everything on my own.

NPS: [*Using a calm voice and nodding to demonstrate she is following the conversation*] I understand, but do you think it's true that you are forgetful
at times, for example in finding the correct words in a conversation? Has this happened occasionally? Or is everything always ok?

E: [*Trying to sound confident and now keeping eye-contact but still fidgeting
with fingers*] I do everything properly. Let's say that I don't remember something, although this is rare, and then I remember it
immediately!

NPS: [*Taking a short pause to leave the message sinking in; and to make
sure the examinee understands the reasons for the assessment*] But then,
if it is as you say, this examination will be simple and short,

there is no reason to worry or get nervous. Maybe your memory is not so good, but even if you sometimes forget something, it is also true that you have no difficulties at home. Is that what you meant?

E: [*Looking moved and no longer fidgeting*] Yes, you've got it!

NPS: [*Looking pleased and enthusiastic to introduce the current assessment and using hands to accompany the message*] Today I am going to suggest something new that you have not done last time. We are going to use a screen to run some of the tasks because this will allow us to collect information about how quick you answer some questions. What do you think?

E: [*Looking hesitant*] It sounds good! But I had a bad night and I may be a bit slow.

NPS: [*Wondering if the examinee may be exaggerating to avoid being tested*] I am sorry to hear that.... However, there is no need to worry about this because we will take it into account.

3.3.4 Example 4. Engaging with an examinee with a depressive attitude (using Setting B, over the phone)

The conversation below is preceded by greetings and the conventional start of the phone conversation.

NPS: [*Sounding welcoming and interested*] So, you are in your house, a more familiar situation than the clinic. Do you prefer it?

E: [*Sounding positive*]. Yes, it is better. But I am aware I am not the same person as I used to be even in my own house.

NPS: [*With a slightly surprised voice*] What do you mean? Tell me a bit more....

E: [*Speaking with a cracking and hesitant voice and sounding hopeless and tearful*] So after the head injury ... my life ... let's say it changed, changed at work, with my wife and also with the children....

NPS: [*Speaking with a calm and soft voice, mirroring the examinee's words showing an understanding of their perspective - 'Theory of mind'*] Do you think *you* changed or *they* changed?

E: [*Sounding nervous, unsure and crying*] I have changed! I can't do anything I used to do before and I am all alone....

NPS: [*Using a compassionate but firm voice to offer the examinee another perspective; a good example of keeping a leading role*] I am sorry to hear that.... Is your family still living with you?... I thought they were supportive when they brought you to the clinic for the examination recently

E: [*Showing positive engagement, steadier voice, and a thoughtful response*] Yes, my wife and children are supportive and they have been taking me to hospital visits regularly.

NPS: [*Sounding positive and assertive; asking a rhetorical question to encourage a positive reply*] Ah good! So your wife and your children took time to take you to the hospital [*Reformulating*] It seems a good thing that all your family wanted to come with you. Why do you think that is? [*Reformulating*]

E: [*Sounding calmer and more engaged, speaking with a balanced voice*] Maybe because they're worried about me.

NPS: [*Sounding confident and providing reassurance*] Then I would say that you are a lucky husband and father because you are surrounded by people who love you.

E: [*Replying in a comfortable voice*] Yes, but I'm not the same person as before and they always have to help me.

NPS: [*Using a firm voice to engage with the examinee; demonstrating leadership role*] Now let's see where your difficulties lie and then we'll see what we can do and I'll also talk to your family.

E: [*With a questioning voice*] What will happen now?

NPS: [*Soft and calm voice*] Let's begin with some tests over the phone. Find a comfortable and quiet place; I will take you through every step. Try to do your best and we'll see how it goes.

The latter two interviews describe two very different situations. In Example 3, the neuropsychologist tried to 'tune in with the examinee' to make her more cooperative, more aware and accepting of her difficulties, and less hostile towards the assessment. In Example 4, the examinee's depressive attitude – which may invalidate the assessment – required continuous evaluation of whether the psychometric examination should be continued.

Although the paraverbal and non-verbal components of these examples cannot be fully illustrated in the text, it is clear that the neuropsychologist's calm and reassuring voice and body language (for Example 3) contributed to the positive interaction with the examinees. In Example 4, the empathy of the neuropsychologist was essential to understand the examinee's state of mind and to allow him to engage in the conversation.

It is also important to appreciate that the neuropsychologist's encouragement and reassurement should not become patronising, since this may make an examinee distrustful and disengaged during the assessment.

3.3.5 Recommendations for remote testing with self-administered modality (using Setting C)

In setting C, as reported above, the examinee carries out the assessment independently from the neuropsychologist. Yet, some simple and well-recognised rules following basic principles of Human-Computer Interaction (HCI, Stuart et al., 1983; Hustak, Krejcar, 2016) should be used at the beginning of the assessment. For instance, it is important to find out how the examinee feels in general and in relation to the tests they are undertaking. Simple graded questions such as "How are you today?", "Are you nervous about the assessment?", can be asked, offering a progressive scale (for example from 1 – low to 10 – high) to provide an answer. Answers can then be incorporated, with the results subsequently analysed by the neuropsychologist.

To maintain a communicative exchange in setting C, it is also important that the examinee is appropriately encouraged throughout the testing, similar to in-person assessments. Therefore, vocal or written messages and feedback such as "Well done!", "Keep going!", "Good job!" should be regularly presented throughout the examination.

As setting C is currently being developed, additional modalities of communicating with examinees are likely to emerge.

4 Psychometric assessment and neuropsychological tests

This chapter introduces some basic psychometrics concepts applied to neuropsychological testing. In particular, it provides a rationale for considering neuropsychological tests as tools that help to evaluate unobservable constructs (e.g., typically cognitive functions), through observable behaviours. After an initial description of tests and measurement, this chapter discusses the concepts of validity and reliability which need to be taken into account when evaluating the usefulness of a neuropsychological test. The final part of the chapter discusses the methodological principles to select tests for the neuropsychological assessment.

4.1 The psychometric assessment and the neuropsychological tests

'Psychometric assessment' here refers to the phase of neuropsychological assessment based on the administration of a series of tests to an examinee, the collection of scores and the interpretation of the results, to help reach a clinical decision. While the use of tests is always recognized as a key aspect of the neuropsychological assessment, the reasons for this importance are not always spelled out.

In short, the primary role of neuropsychological testing is to provide structured settings to observe the behaviour of the examinee, overcoming the limitations of a qualitative assessment based solely on the clinician's observations and subjective judgments. Neuropsychological tests provide the clinician with a unique opportunity to analyse the ability of an examinee, in performing specific behaviours such as calculations, writing, drawing, recalling, or learning new information. In particular, neuropsychological tests critically provide methodologically rigorous support to elicit observable behaviours, designed to identify cognitive impairments and to help reaching a

DOI: 10.4324/9781003195221-4

neuropsychological diagnosis. Tests can also be used for other reasons, for example for monitoring examinees' performance over time, to assess if they changed after rehabilitation or following a relevant event, such as a neurosurgical operation.

Chapters 4 to 7 address all the major theoretical and practical aspects of psychometric assessment in clinical neuropsychology, that is, the use of scores obtained through neuropsychological tests. This topic is fundamental for the work of the neuropsychologist since an incorrect use of tests or a misinterpretation of the results may lead to an incorrect neuropsychological diagnosis and errors on the clinical classification, diagnosis and prognosis inferred from the examinee's neuropsychological results.

4.2 A definition of a neuropsychological test

Although many types of tests can be used in the neuropsychological assessment, here 'neuropsychological test' refers to a *performance test*, in which the examinee is required to use a cognitive ability to accomplish some tasks. These are different from other tests (for example, personality tests) in which there is no performance involved, but rather a self-report. A classic definition of a psychological test (and that we adopt here for neuropsychological tests) is the one by the psychologist Lee Cronbach, who largely influenced Test Theory with his contributions:

> A test is a systematic procedure for observing a person's behaviour and describing it with the aid of a numerical scale or a category-sistem.
>
> (Cronbach, 1970, p. 26)

This definition captures three essential characteristics of a neuropsychological test:

1 "*A test is a systematic procedure*": The term 'systematic procedure' indicates a procedure characterised by a well-defined sequence of events. For example, all tests are accompanied by detailed instructions to the examinee, the material to be used (e.g., pictures, cards, tokens), and how it should be organised (e.g., placed on the table in front of the examinee). If specific devices or software are used, the procedure for using it should also be specified.

2 "*for observing a person's behaviour*": Tests provide a structured setting which elicits and reveals behaviours that may act as windows into the examinee's cognitive functioning. In the case of a computer-

based test, no 'observation' as such can be made, however the collected data are used for examining a specific behaviour;

However, data collected via software overlook relevant qualitative details, compared to the traditional human-based neuropsychological assessment.

3   *"and describing it with the aid of a numerical scale or a category-sistem"*: Any neuropsychological test includes rules that allow us to classify an examinee's performance and often to categorise it using a score. This is the feature that makes neuropsychological tests a fundamental tool for the neuropsychologist. Scores may require a proactive role from the neuropsychologist, for instance in the case of paper-and-pencil tests (which require the agreement across different scorers, see section 4.5.5.1), or can be automatically calculated by software or a device.

Cronbach's definition captures three key aspects, but does not take into account the fact that neuropsychology is almost never focused on behaviour *per se*, but rather on the information that this behaviour can provide about cognitive functioning, often centred around a specific theoretical construct.[1] For example, let's consider the Digit Span (Weschler, 1939; Monaco et al., 2013), a test measuring short-term memory capacity, whereby an examinee is required to listen to and then recall sequences of numbers of increasing length (for example, '5 3 2' followed by '6 8 4 5' and so on). Here the examinee's observed behaviour is related to the number of digits recalled, although the assessment is focused on the cognitive function underlying it, in this case the examinee's short-term memory. The behaviour is a *proxy*: something that can be observed and that allows us to measure a psychological construct that cannot be directly observed.

The relationship between a construct and its proxy is never perfect, and other aspects than the construct of interest may affect performance on a test. Consider, for example, the examinee's motivation. If this is very low, this may affect performance which will inevitably be poor, regardless of the cognitive function measured. Similar effects may be generated by excessive anxiety, which may affect performance even when the cognitive function measured is intact. In addition to these collateral variables, such as mood, motivation, and fatigue, performance on a neuropsychological test can also be affected by other cognitive functions of no interest. For example, a severe impairment in attention, could lead to loss of focus during a language test, leading to impaired performance. A key assumption of the Interpretative

Approach presented here is that associating a test score to a specific cognitive function (or construct) in clinical neuropsychology implies an interpretation which is related to the active role of the neuropsychologist (see sections 1.1 and 6.3).

To summarise this important concept: neuropsychological tests aim to indirectly measure specific cognitive functions (abstract, unobservable constructs) through observable behaviours. In turn the observed test behaviour reflects the cognitive function measured by that test, likely to be influenced by other spurious factors, such as motivation, anxiety and others. A key role of the neuropsychologist is to minimise the impact of these factors on performance, or to be able to quantify their contribution in an implicit manner. For example, whenever we interpret a memory test as actually measuring memory we are implicitly assuming that all other factors (anxiety, mood, motivation, other cognitive functions, etc.) have not played a relevant role in the performance[2]. This relationship is illustrated in Figure 4.1 and further expanded in section 4.3.

The box labelled "Other variables" refers to spurious and undesired variables that may affect behaviour and in turn the final score. This may occur independently from the construct of interest, thus confounding the inference of a construct from the observed behaviour.

The dashed grey line represents the measurement: representing a construct with a score. Finally, the neuropsychologist interprets the scores (see section 6.2).

4.2.1 *Digital (computerised) neuropsychological tests*

At the time of writing this book, despite the wide availability of computers or tablets, digital testing is still limited and most neuropsychological tests are still paper-and-pencil (Bilder & Reise, 2019; Russell, 2011). There are different possible reasons for this, including cost of the devices, the higher flexibility of paper-and-pencil tests (e.g., they may be more easily interrupted and restarted), and the reluctance some people have to use technology (for example for older examinees, but even from some clinicians).

Critically, though, all the considerations made for paper-and-pencil tests hold for digital tests too, with a few exceptions (e.g., the score attribution, see Figure 4.1, and section 6.1). As for paper-and-pencil tests, digital tests allow the collection of information on relevant behaviours of the examinee, and interpreting and integrating them with other available data.

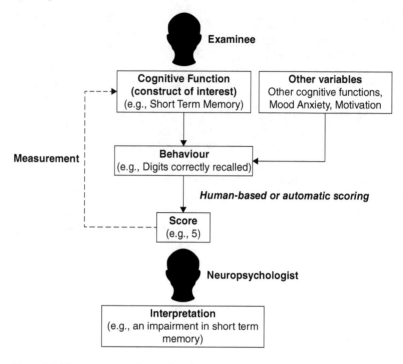

Figure 4.1 Measurements obtained with a neuropsychological test and their interpretation. The relation between a cognitive function assessed with a
test (construct, white rectangle on the top) and the corresponding score
(rectangle at the bottom). The cognitive construct influences the examinee's behaviour, that through human-based or automatic scoring, is
transformed to a number, that is the test score.

4.3 Measurement in neuropsychology and test development

A crucial concept related to the use of tests is that of *measurement*. Since
the use of tests is typically associated with obtaining a numerical value or
score, tests are often considered measurement tools. For instance, there
are neuropsychological tests that *measure* memory, attention, independence in daily life and so on. A common definition of measurement in
psychology is one proposed about 60 years ago by Stanley Smith Stevens:

> We may say that measurement, in the broadest sense, is defined as
> the assignment of numerals to objects or events according to rules.
> (Stevens, 1946)

This definition, which has been widely adopted in the psychological sciences, is also the most used (at least implicitly) for neuropsychological tests: for each test there is a set of rules that transform performance into a numerical value, the test score. There are other conceptualizations of measurement that differ from Stevens' one.[3] The most famous alternative in psychology is related to the "Rasch models" (Stone, Wright, & Stenner, 1999; Bilder & Reise, 2018), an approach today known as "Item Response Theory", IRT (Kline, 2005; Thomas et al., 2018). In IRT a measurement implies precise mathematical properties (e.g., monotonicity, identifiability of item parameters, ect.) present in a test in the relationship between scores (i.e., numbers) and what is being measured (i.e., the theoretical construct). Dealing with IRT models from a mathematical point of view is beyond the scope of this chapter. Most available neuropsychological tests are not based on the assumptions of the IRT models, but are based on the so-called Classical Test Theory – CTT (for further discussion see Kline, 2005). The choice of a theoretical approach in the development of a neuropsychological test (CTT or IRT) determines how the test is built and the information that is available about the test in the textbook or scientific article in which it is illustrated (as with the concepts of reliability and validity; see section 4.5).

In CTT, the criteria defining a measurement are less strict compared to those of IRT and they are compatible with a definition of measurement such as Stevens' considered. A feature of tests developed according to CTT is that a different patterns on test items can easily lead to the same overall score. This is a crucial issue because a critical aim of a measurement is to obtain a value that can unequivocally represent the same property. Metaphorically speaking, it would be like having a weight scale that sometimes does not measure weight but other properties (for example, height). A concrete example of a test developed according to CTT can be helpful in understanding the problem.

Consider the Montreal Cognitive Assessment – MoCA (Nasreddine et al., 2005), a very popular neuropsychological test built according to the principles of CTT. The final score of MoCA is the sum of the scores obtained in a series of items that meet the requirements assessed in the development phase of the test (e.g., having a sufficiently high value in the internal consistency see section 4.5.3). The MoCA consists of a set of heterogeneous items, spanning spatial orientation, short-term memory, verbal fluency and other cognitive abilities. The final score, which can be between 0 and 30, is the sum of the scores in all the items that make up the test. Now, consider two hypothetical examinees to whom the MoCA is administered, both with a final score of 20. The first may be because they performed poorly in many items of the test, the second examinee because they performed poorly only in two items, e.g., short-term memory and spatio-temporal orientation items. In this case two identical scores (both examinees scoring 20) correspond to two different performances, likely underlying distinct features of cognitive functioning. This aspect (and potential limitation) is not *per se* incorrect, but is the consequence of the theoretical assumptions used to build the test, of the CTT and of a definition of measurement such as Stevens'. If developed within the IRT framework, the above case would be extremely unlikely (the methods of building measurement tools aim to prevent the possibility that the same score is related to very different patterns of performances). Following the IRT criteria to construct a test, the chance that different performance patterns may lead to similar scores is avoided. A test with these characteristics would simply not be considered a measurement tool. Specifically, in the basic formulation of IRT, a test should include items of varying difficulty, and the probability of answering an item correctly should be proportional to its difficulty and to the ability of an examinee (Bond & Fox, 2007).

Knowing the principles on which a test is based can be very important to a clinician in order to interpret the results of the test. IRT-based tests are more rigorous than real measurement scales, as they measure neuropsychological constructs and rank an examinee with respect to that measure (see, for example Prieto et al., 2010).

Despite the methodological rigour of IRT, the neuropsychological tests developed with CTT are in some cases equally effective in clinical practice (Hula et al., 2006). One might ask why neuropsychological tests are not always created in accordance with IRT, since these models are more sophisticated and theoretically more rigorous. The reason is probably both historical and practical: developing a test according to IRT is more laborious and expensive, requires much more theoretical knowledge and does not necessarily lead to a satisfactory result. Moreover, results deriving from the CTT or IRT approach are often very similar (Hula et al., 2006). As the large majority of neuropsychological tests are developed in accordance with CTT, in the remainder of the chapter (and the textbook) we will always refer to this approach. We will also assume it is legitimate to say that a test 'measures' cognitive functions or neuropsychological constructs. The clinical neuropsychologist should consider that in CTT-based tests (especially those measuring very general constructs) the same score may correspond to different performances (and therefore different cognitive functioning).

4.4 Constructs investigated in the neuropsychological assessment

The neuropsychological assessment (and so the neuropsychological tests) typically investigates several constructs at different hierarchical levels. This heterogeneity reflects the history of clinical neuropsychology and its multidisciplinarity (Russell, 2011), which led to different approaches, each stressing distinct aspects or features to be assessed. In this section, a list of constructs measured by neuropsychological tests will be first provided, followed by some general considerations on the constructs covered in neuropsychological tests.

- Most neuropsychological tests assess cognitive functions, i.e., well-defined theoretical constructs from cognitive neuropsychology (Riddoch & Humphreys 1994). Take for example the Oxford Cognitive Screening (Demeyere et al., 2015). This screening battery contains several subtests measuring different cognitive functions, such as short-term memory (Digit span), working memory (Interference memory test), abstraction skills (Abstraction test), and others. Typically, studies from cognitive neuroscience investigate the neural correlates of such constructs, in terms of specific brain areas or networks (Goldstein & McNeil, 2012; Ponsford, 2004).
- Some tests measure constructs originating from educational and clinical psychology, such as for example intelligence scales (Wechsler, 1939). Currently, some IQ-based tests are used in neuropsychological assessment as clinical tools (e.g., Raven's matrices; Raven 2008).
- Some tests used in the neuropsychological assessment do not measure specific cognitive functions, but more broad constructs. An example is provided by screening tests on global cognitive functioning (e.g., the MMSE – Folstein, Folstein, & McHuges, 1975; MoCA – Nasreddine et al., 2005; FAB – Dubois et al., 2000). These tests are quite common in clinical practice because of their capacity to provide valuable information about an examinee in a very short time.
- Beside screening tests, many test batteries provide global scores used to describe the general intellectual/cognitive functioning of the examinees (e.g., Repeatable Battery for Neuropsychological Status, RBANS, cit. or the Assessment of Pragmatic Abilities and

Cognitive Substrates, APACS – Arcara & Bambini, 2016). These constructs, measured by global scores, are very different those formulated in cognitive neuropsychology, for instance 'short-term memory' and are used to provide a quick picture of the examinee and a clinical classification (e.g., examinees with severe dementia, or with Mild Cognitive Impairment).

- In neuropsychological assessment, it is often crucial to obtain additional information about an examinee through questionnaires which are not strictly *neuropsychological tests* (according to our definition, see section 4.3), as they are not performance tests. Questionnaires can be administered directly to the examinee themselves or in some cases to a carer. Such questionnaires can measure characteristics different to cognitive functions, and which may have an important influence on performance. A relevant characteristic to be measured is mood, or more specifically depressive symptoms; in elderly examinees these can be measured by means of the Geriatric Depression Scale (Yesavage et al., 1988). Important information in the investigation of cognition and for diagnostic purposes is the measure of cognitive reserve (for example, with the CRI-q – Nucci et al., 2012).

- Other constructs that can be investigated during the neuropsychological assessment refer to more ecological and daily living activities, such as driving, dressing, or managing one's own finances. These constructs may be assessed by functional 'scales', like the Activities of Daily Living (ADL – Katz et al., 1963), Instrumental Activity of Daily Living (IADL – Lawton & Brody, 1969) or actual neuropsychological tests, which involve the use of performance tests, like other neuropsychological tests (e.g., Numerical Activities of Daily Living, NADL – Semenza et al., 2013) or Numerical Activities of DAily Living – Financial (NADL-F – Arcara et al., 2017). Using tests that measure these constructs allows the clinician to answer questions relevant for the prognosis of an examinee and often related to their independence (such as "will the examinee be independent in daily life", "will the examinee be able to drive?"). Tests on functional abilities are limited in assessing the actual ability to perform an activity rather than explaining the reasons for not being able to perform that activity. For example, a bad performance on a test that evaluates driving skills may indicate that the examinee is unable to drive, although there could be many underlying reasons (problems with attention or psychomotor speed, visual or motor deficits). Hypotheses about the reasons for the impairment can be inferred from the combined interpretation of the evidence collected in the neuropsychological assessment (see section 6.2). Some of these tests can be classified as scales (e.g., IADL) while others are performance tests, and so can be classified as actual neuropsychological tests (e.g., NADL-F).

• Finally, some common neuropsychological tests originated specifically in the context of clinical neuropsychology. Although they do not measure single and specific cognitive constructs (at least not according to up-to-date cognitive models), they are widely used for their clinical potential. For example, the Token Test which was designed more than 50 years ago by De Renzi & Vignolo (1962) assesses language comprehension skills, rather than measuring a specific cognitive function (it is for example related to working memory, but also to visual recognition skills, spatial attention, etc.). Despite its 'age', the Token Test has recently been converted into a digital version and translation into numerous languages given its easy use and clinical relevance (Bastiaanse et al., 2016). Another example is the Clock Drawing Test, in which an examinee draws a clock with the hands in a specific position (Critchley, 1953). Several cognitive functions rather than a specific one are measured (such as praxic abilities, planning abilities, memory retrieval, etc., Pinto & Peters, 2009).

Tests such as the Token Test, or the Clock Drawing Test are typically used for their ability to signal the presence of a potential cognitive disorder rather than their ability to give accurate information on specific cognitive functions (Pinto & Peters, 2009).

To summarise, neuropsychological assessment involves the use of tests that measure constructs at very different levels. During the assessment, the neuropsychologist may integrate the information provided by tests measuring different constructs (see the list above), but should not forget that they may tap on different features (and some on different hierarchical levels) of cognitive functioning.

Such richness of opportunities in constructs to be assessed during a neuropsychological assessment has important pros and cons. On the upside, the neuropsychologist can rely on a *plethora* of possibilities to investigate specific aspects of the cognitive functioning of an examinee. On the downside, this richness reflects the lack of agreement on what is supposed to be assessed and measured during a neuropsychological assessment. Even if scientific associations or consensus papers tend to provide indications of the domains to be tested and the test to be used (e.g., Strong et al., 2017, for Consensus Criteria for Amyotrophic Lateral Sclerosis), there is not a clear and widespread agreement on what is meant to be measured and assessed. Hence, the final choices depend largely on the context in which the neuropsychologist will work (and even the country). This is in contrast to what happens, for example, in the medical field whereby there is a worldwide agreement on how to assess some medical conditions. To give a more concrete example, for the medical condition of Mellitus Diabete it is widely agreed that the diagnosis should be based on blood samples, and in particular on tests such as the fasting plasma glucose (FPG) test, the haemoglobin A1c (A1c) test, and an oral glucose tolerance test (OGTT). Any physician working in this field (no matter the country or the hospital) would likely rely on such tests to reach a diagnosis. In the neuropsychological field, on the contrary, an analogous agreement cannot be found, even for very popular neuropsychological disorders such as Alzheimer's disease. Indeed, the neuropsychological diagnosis of Alzheimer's (see also Chapter 8, for considerations on the neuropsychological diagnosis), can be based on different tests that change across countries, or even within the same country, across different hospitals or centres. This lack of agreement also pertains to the usefulness of the test in relation to the construct measured, and it is almost impossible to find shared criteria that define when a neuropsychological test must be considered obsolete. While in the medical field it is common to witness evolution of diagnostic tests over the time (and old tests are replaced from new one), at the time of publishing of this textbook there is no evidence of neuropsychological tests that are deprecated from clinical practice because they proved to be inadequate, or assessing obsolete construct (see Dodrill, 1997 for some criticism to the theoretical development of clinical neuropsychology). Recent advances in neuroscience, for example, are suggesting the adoption of different concepts of cognitive ontologies (Poldrack & Yarkoni, 2016), and this may be extended to the field of clinical neuropsychology, leading to the use of different cognitive domains and tests (Masina et al., 2022). However, a likely scenario is that these new constructs will be investigated during the assessment together with older ones.

Going deeper into this topic is beyond the aim of this textbook, but the important point here is that the neuropsychologist should be aware of such lack of agreement and the potential implications of it (examinations conducted in different centres may reach different conclusions, just on the basis of the different tests used). There is no simple way to tackle this issue, as it appears to be the consequence of the lack of a dominant scientific paradigm in both cognitive psychology and in neuropsychology, which led to the flourishing of different perspectives with no well-defined, widely accepted view.

4.5 The main properties of a test: validity and reliability

When deciding to use a neuropsychological test, it is always essential to evaluate two qualities of the test: its reliability and its validity.

Validity is the quality of an instrument to actually measure the construct it wants to measure, while *reliability* indicates the consistency of the measures provided by the test.

In order to reach a correct neuropsychological diagnosis, it is fundamental to use tests that are valid for a specific interpretation and with high reliability; that is, a high precision in scores. In this section the concepts of validity and reliability will be defined in detail and the consequences of using unreliable tests, or for purposes for which they are not valid, will be discussed.

4.5.1 Validity

There are many possible definitions of 'validity'. The one proposed by an American consortium of psychology associations is particularly clear:

The validity of a test is "the degree to which all accumulated evidence supports the interpretation of test scores in accordance with the purpose of the test" (AERA, APA, NCME, 1999, p. 11, cited in Urbina, 2004).

This definition points to three crucial aspects about the validity of a test.

1   The first is that it is irrelevant to say that a test is 'valid' or not in general. Rather, the scores of a test may or may not be valid *for a certain interpretation* (or for more than one). For example, the Digit Span score may be valid for measuring short-term memory, but it is not valid for measuring long-term memory. Hence beware that the statement "you can use this test in the neuropsychological assessment, it is proven to be valid" is meaningless: the validity depends on the interpretation one draws from the test scores.

2   The second crucial aspect is that validation (i.e., the process of establishing the validity of a test) is not an all-or-nothing process but rather a quality that lies along a continuum and is accumulated. A test may be more valid than another for a certain purpose (e.g., to measure working memory).

3   The third is that a test's scores may be valid for different purposes. For example, the MoCA in its original Canadian version has been shown to be valid for discriminating between MCI, Alzheimer's

examinees and healthy participants (Nasreddine et al., 2005), but another research group has shown that it can also be used to predict the presence of cognitive deficits after a stroke (Salvadori et al., 2013).

Historically, different types of validity have been identified and different classifications (and hierarchical organisations) have been proposed (see Cronbach, 1970). A recent view on validity (Urbina, 2004) traces all its features to construct validity, defining the term 'construct' as any psychological concept. In particular there would be three different aspects of construct validity: content validity, convergent-divergent validity, and criterion validity.

4.5.2 Content validity

Content validity refers to the property of a test to be made of items that encompass all the relevant aspects related to the construct that the test aims to measure. For example, a neuropsychological test that aims to assess general reading skills and that only includes single-word items (and no sentences or longer text) is unlikely to have sufficient content validity, as many aspects related to reading and relevant to assess reading abilities are not included.

Although formulas for quantifying content validity have been proposed (Lawshe, 1975), the content validity of a test is most often assessed qualitatively according to perspective of the theory a test is developed from, and in relation to the choice of its items. This information can be found in the test's manual or in the scientific article presenting it. It is the responsibility of the neuropsychologist to informally assess whether a test has sufficient content validity for a given purpose.

4.5.3 Convergent-divergent validity

The term convergent-divergent validity refers to several properties of a test. First of all, it indicates that the items of the test are consistent in measuring the same construct and correlate with each other (this is usually assessed by means of Internal Consistency and Factor Analysis of the items). It also means a test score correlates with other test scores measuring the same construct, and at the same time does not correlate with tests measuring other constructs. For example, in order to be able to say that a test is selectively measuring memory (and have convergent-divergent validity in this sense), its score should correlate with other memory tests and should not correlate (or correlate weakly) with tests on visuospatial attention.

Within the concept of construct validity falls also the property of a test to reveal experimental features that are in line with theoretical expectations. For example, in a test assessing communication skills, aphasic examinees are likely to score worse than non-aphasic participants. An experimental study confirming this pattern would provide further support to the validity of the test measuring communication skills. Showing age and education effects consistent with what is expected from a theoretical perspective is considered further evidence in support of convergent-divergent validity.

In relation to validity, two relevant type of data analyses are the *internal consistency* analysis and *factor* analysis, the first studying the relationship between items of the same test, the second between different subtests that make up a test battery. Internal consistency measures the coherence between items in a test, which is needed to be meaningfully integrated within the test. The most common index of internal consistency is Cronbach's alpha, whose value ranges between 0 and 1, where '0' indicates a test based on items totally independent of each other, and '1' where the items are instead perfectly related to each other (in fact too related, becoming practically indistinguishable). A consistency index of at least 0.7 is desirable for a neuropsychological test (Slick, 2006a), but it is very common to find tests with lower internal consistency (about 0.6, Strauss, Sherman, & Spreen, 2006). The internal consistency index is sometimes reported as a quality related to test reliability rather than validity. This is because internal consistency is a quality that straddles the two concepts of validity and reliability. Note also that many alternatives have been proposed to Cronbach's alpha, due to the some limitations of this measure of internal consistency (Trizano-Heromosilla & Alvarado, 2016).

Factor analysis is another important analysis used to evaluate the convergent-divergent validity of a test. In the context of neuropsychological testing, factor analysis can be defined as an analysis that simultaneously investigates possible correlations between test scores and attempts to extract latent variables that explain these correlations. A factor analysis can be done at the level of a test's item (with a purpose similar to internal consistency) or between the subtests that make up a test battery. This aims at checking that the relationship between scores is meaningful and provides support to the validity of the test in its complexity. Consider a hypothetical test battery that includes three tests on short-term memory and four tests on executive functions. To support the construct validity of the test, a factor analysis performed on the subtests should identify two factors (latent variables): a latent variable related to short-term memory (capturing correlations among the three short-term memory tests) and a latent variable related to executive functions (capturing correlations among the four executive function tests). This hypothetical result would confirm validity because it would be the expected result if the tests measured what they were intended to measure. In real life of course results tend to be more complicated and a certain amount of experience and theoretical knowledge is required to be able to interpret the goodness of the results of a factor analysis in the context of the validity of neuropsychological tests.

4.5.4 Criterion validity

Criterion validity is the property of a test to provide results that are closely related to an external criterion. An external criterion is an observable indicator obtained separately from the test. The criterion may be qualitative, such as the presence-absence of a pathological condition, or it may be quantitative, such as the score on another test considered to be a gold standard against which the test in question is validated.

Qualitative criteria, such as the presence or absence of a pathological condition, are very important in many neuropsychological tests and are discussed extensively in Chapter 7.

To provide an example of a quantitative criterion let's consider an hypothetical short test that aims at estimating IQ. In order to have criterion validity this must correlate with longer and extensive IQ tests. In this case the external criterion is given by a standard IQ test, which is a score, and criterion validity can be expressed by a correlation or another value that expresses how well the test provides similar information to the external criterion.

Tests based on criterion validity do not necessarily measure a specific theoretical construct, but focus on predicting membership of a certain clinical condition, or the development of a disease. In this sense they differ from tests that measure specific constructs (such as short-term memory) and certain measurement-related problems become less relevant. In this case the effectiveness of the test is often assessed purely on predictive ability and it is relatively less important to understand what is being measured by the numbers used (Capitani & Laiacona, 1999).

The list of validity types presented in this chapter represents only a part of all validity types, but it is the most relevant for clinical neuropsychology. Please refer to other textbooks for a more in-depth discussion (e.g., Urbina, 2004).

4.5.5 Reliability

Reliability is the quality of a test to provide consistent scores across different measurements. For this reason, it can be conceived as the accuracy of a test.

There are generally two main types of reliability used in neuropsychological testing, which refer to the assessment of two types of score consistency: inter-rater reliability and test-retest reliability.

4.5.5.1 Inter-rater reliability

Inter-rater reliability is a measure of the consistency with which different examiners rate the same performance of the same examinee. It is usually expressed by a coefficient, the intraclass correlation, which varies between 0 and 1, where '0' indicates complete inconsistency between scores and '1' indicates full consistency between the scores of two or more examiners. A low inter-rater reliability score means that for the same performance, two neuropsychologists may provide quite different scores. This would obviously represent a major limitation in the possibilities of using the test and in the inferences that can be drawn from its scores. There are no clear-cut thresholds on what should be a sufficient inter-rater reliability score for a test, but values greater than 0.60 are desirable (Slick, 2006).

Low inter-rater reliability may be the consequence of unclear or ambiguous instructions for test scoring; it is often associated with tests addressing complex and varied behaviour resulting in ambiguous scoring. Note that in the case of automatic scoring, as in digital testing, inter-rater agreement has little or no importance, as the same algorithm would provide the same score to the same performance.

4.5.5.2 Test-retest reliability

Test-retest reliability is the correlation of two measurements with the same test by the same examiner on the same individual after a time interval in which no change is assumed to have occurred.

Test-retest reliability is often calculated by means of a correlation (Pearson's correlation) between the scores on the first and second measurement, with values varying between -1 and 1. Positive values in the correlation generally indicate a desirable condition for a test in which high scores on the first measurement are matched by high scores on the second measurement, and low scores on the first measurement are matched by low scores on the second measurement. Negative values in test-retest reliability indicate a (very unlikely) condition in which the scores have an inverse correlation, i.e., those who score high on the first measurement tend to score low on the second and vice versa. Correlations close to zero indicate no relationship between scores on the first and second measurements, suggesting a large influence of errors that make the test very inaccurate.

As with inter-rater reliability, there is no precise threshold value for considering a test with sufficient test-retest reliability, but the value should be at least 0.70 (Slick, 2006). However, some neuropsychological tests do not meet these criteria (see Slick, 2006). In such cases it is necessary to use and interpret the scores from this tests carefully and with caution.

An important aspect related to test-retest is that it simply indicates the correlation between two measurements rather than the stability of a measurement over time. Specifically, high test-retest reliability indicates that there are few random errors (i.e., random fluctuations) of scores between two measurements, but it is not informative about systematic fluctuations. An example of systematic fluctuation is the so-called 'practice effect', which refers to the common situation in neuropsychology whereby a second measurement always tends to have better scores than the first. An (extreme) case in which all subjects score exactly ten points higher in the second measurement than in the first would lead to perfect test-retest reliability (i.e., 1). In this case there would be no random fluctuations, only a systematic fluctuation, which is not captured by the formula for test-retest reliability (i.e., Pearson's correlation). This aspect will be discussed in detail in section 5.3.

4.5.6 The relationship between reliability and validity

Reliability and validity are the two main qualities of a test, and a neuropsychologist should be aware of the qualities of the tests they use in clinical practice. It is important to emphasise that reliability and validity are dissociable due to the nature of what they assess (see Figure 4.2). A test may be very accurate (thus very reliable), but not very valid for a certain interpretation (Figure 4.2, panel c): for instance, a short-term memory test may be very reliable, but not valid for assessing memory in everyday life.

Although it is theoretically possible for an unreliable test to be valid (see Figure 4.2, panel d), unreliable tests are always also poorly valid for any inference: since they are extremely imprecise, one can hardly say that one is measuring anything with such tests.

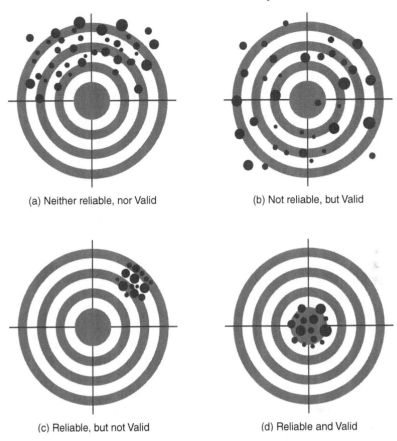

(a) Neither reliable, nor Valid (b) Not reliable, but Valid

(c) Reliable, but not Valid (d) Reliable and Valid

Figure 4.2 Relationship between validity and reliability of a test. The centre represents the construct that is aimed to measure. Black circles indicate hypothetical results of several repeated measurements (e.g., several measurements, using the same test, on the same examinee). Scattered circles far from the center indicate a test that is neither reliable nor valid (panel a). Scattered circles that are on average in the center indicate the hypothetical condition of an unreliable but valid test. In this case however, the test is often not considered valid, because of the inaccuracy that undermines the validity in measuring the construct. Circles close to each other but far from the center indicate a reliable, but invalid test (panel c). Circles close together and in the center indicate a reliable and valid test (panel d).

4.5.7 Cognitive fluctuations and reliability

An important aspect related to reliability concerns the stability of cognitive functions in the case of cognitive impairment. Many neuropsychological conditions are indeed characterised by fluctuations (across days or even within the same day), affecting the reliability of the measures (that are typically obtained in healthy participants, whose performance is much more stable). This increased intra-individual variability in performance, often defined as 'cognitive fluctuations', is common knowledge among clinicians, and it is also confirmed in different pathologies (e.g., in Alzheimer's Dementia – Trachsel et al., 2015; in Lewy & Body dementia – Matar et al., 2020; in neglect – Klinke et al., 2016; Pitteri et al., 2017).

With this premise, neuropsychological assessment should be considered just as a 'photograph' of a potential unstable state, at risk of providing a wrong picture. In particular, an above cut-off performance see section 5.3 may be observed even in the case of an existing cognitive impairment, for instance if it is accompanied by important fluctuations, and if the examination occurs during a moment of 'good' functioning.

A solution to this issue could be to repeat the measurements more than once. Similarly to medical tests that can be repeated many times and at home (like Holter testing for blood pressure), an interesting opportunity for clinical neuropsychology is provided by self-testing software that can be used by the examinees at home (see section 1.2 on Settings). Unlike medical examinations, practice effects in neuropsychological assessments should nevertheless be taken into account (see sections 4.5.5.2 and 6.3). Far from being a substitute of direct assessment, the information gathered via remote multiple assessment over time may provide further evidence that may be used to reach a neuropsychological diagnosis.

4.5.8 Validity and reliability information during the assessment

A common problem related to validity and reliability is that they are often perceived as abstract psychometric concepts related to test development, with limited utility for the actual clinical practice. For instance, a recent review for Italian tests showed how these properties are often overlooked in many screening tests (Aiello et al., 2021). Typically, if a test is published in a peer-reviewed journal, or by a publishing-house, it is inferred by the neuropsychologist that it can be used in clinical practice, without further considerations. This is a common but incorrect practice. Validity and reliability of a test provide important information available to the neuropsychologist to interpret the evidence collected during the assessment.

For example, let's suppose an examinee is evaluated after six months for a suspect of dementia. Compared to a previous assessment, the examinee obtains a slightly lower score in a memory test. This memory test, however, has quite low test-retest reliability (e.g., 0.55). In this case the neuropsychologist could take into account this aspect and weight properly the evidence about this test. In this specific case, the change in performance may be related to fluctuations of the scores due to test properties, rather than on a real change in the examinee's memory (see also section 5.7.1). It would be easier if such decisions of whether a test is satisfactory or not are guided by objective thresholds or rules. Defining such rules is however not simple, as it will be explained in the next paragraph.

4.5.9 When is a neuropsychological test good enough to be used?

The previous paragraphs discussed the main properties that define the quality of a test, especially validity and reliability (except from normative data, see Chapter 5) and provide suggestions on the thresholds to be used to decide whether a test has satisfactory properties or not (e.g., test-retest reliability higher than 0.7).

These thresholds should be considered as rules-of-thumb (Slick, 2006), and unfortunately there is no widespread consensus in the neuropsychological community on what thresholds or criteria define if a neuropsychological test is good enough to be included in an assessment.

These arbitrary rules or principles can only be reached by the consensus of the scientific community, since there are no objective ways to decide when a test should be used or not. However, some tests have better properties than others, and the concepts provided in this chapter may help the neuropsychologist to make an informed choice in selecting the tests for their assessment.

The topic of test selection is discussed in the next section.

4.6 The selection of tests

Choosing the tests that will be used to assess the examinee is a fundamental aspect of psychometric assessment and so of the neuropsychological assessment. There are two types of occasions on which the neuropsychologist has to choose the tests: choosing the available tests to own and that could be used in the assessment (buying them, or, if they are freely available, printing them and preparing the materials); and choosing the tests to use for a specific assessment.

Within the neuropsychologist's 'toolbox' it is fundamental to include tests with certain qualities: the tests must have scientific proof of validity for the interpretations that will then be made from the results and must be reliable (see section 5.3); the tests must have adequate normative data, if the aim is to assess cognitive deficit (see Chapter 5), and should have adequate methods to assess significant change, if measuring over time is the aim of the assessment (see section 5.3). In general, the neuropsychologist should consider using only tests with proven scientific qualities, and should prefer tests with the best properties.

In addition to choosing the available tests, the neuropsychologist has to choose which tests to use in a specific assessment or the neuropsychological assessment routine. There are three forms of testing:

a   Fixed battery
b   Flexible battery
c   Fixed screening battery plus ad-hoc tests

Each has its own advantages and disadvantages:

a   The use of a fixed battery indicates that each examinee is assessed with the same set of tests, regardless of the diagnostic questions or information already available to the neuropsychologist. Generally, the tests of a fixed battery tend to assess every aspect and facet of cognitive functioning, in a rather in-depth manner. The use of a fixed battery approach appears to be very popular when enough time is available to assess each examinee (this could require several hours, possibly divided into separate days to avoid excessive fatigue). The main advantage of this method is that it allows a comprehensive examination of the examinee's cognitive functioning regardless of the examiner's assumptions. The disadvantage is that the assessment can generally become too time-consuming and often involves the administration of many irrelevant tests (Goldstein, 1997).
b   The use of a flexible battery indicates that each examinee is assessed with different tests, depending on the diagnostic or evaluative question. The use of a flexible battery is associated with the assessment method known as "hypothesis testing" (Goldstein, 1997). The neuropsychologist formulates a series of hypotheses on

the examinee's cognitive state and tries to refute or verify them through the use of appropriate tests. In this method, the assessment takes the form of a series of questions (e.g., "Does the examinee have a memory deficit?"). These questions may initially come from the neuropsychological interview and clinical observation of the examinee. As the assessment proceeds, the results of the tests used may therefore confirm the hypotheses, falsify them or suggest new ones. The advantage of using a flexible battery is that it is versatile and less time-consuming as compared to a fixed battery. The main disadvantage of this procedure is the risk of excessive subjectivity. The hypotheses of the neuropsychologist, given the active role in test selection, may bias the investigation by focusing on certain aspects and neglecting others.

c The third approach is situated between the other two and has been called "individual-centred normative approach", and involves the use of a short fixed battery (for screening) followed by other tests, flexibly chosen starting from the initial clinical question (Goldstein, 1997) or from the results of the screening battery. The battery can be an already existing battery (e.g., Brief-Repeatable-Battery for multiple sclerosis, Rao & the Cognitive Function Study Group of the National Multiple Sclerosis Society, 1990; Boringa et al., 2001), or can be built by the neuropsychologist by select-ing a small collection of tests. Following the administration of the screening battery, a hypothesis-testing investigation takes place: the neuropsychologist formulates specific questions and tries to obtain further specific information by performing specific tests. This approach has the advantages and disadvantages of the fixed battery and flexible battery approaches. An example of what could be the psychometric assessment using this approach is the follow-ing: suppose an examinee is assessed, reported by family members for problems with numbers and for some signs of cognitive impair-ment. An initial test with a screening battery reveals a memory deficit and a picture compatible with Mild Cognitive Impairment (Petersen, 2011; 2014). In order to answer more precisely the rele-vant question posed by the examinees, further specific tests could be administered that could answer the specific question on the use of money (e.g., for using subtests of the NADL-F see Arcara et al., 2017).

The different ways of choosing neuropsychological tests and how to conduct the examination reflect two schools of thought, present in both neurology and neuropsychology: the 'comprehensive-school' and the 'hypothesis-driven school' (Rae-Grant & Parsons, 2014). While the first approach – fixed battery – fully reflects the comprehensive school, and the flexible battery approach reflects the hypothesis-driven school, the approach with screening battery and ad-hoc tests can be seen as partly embracing both positions.

The choice of a specific approach is linked to both theoretical choices and practical considerations, and on the aims of the neuropsychological assessment. For assessment with the aim of making a comprehensive picture of the examinee's cognitive deficits, a fixed battery approach could be more suitable, especially when a multicentre study of new pathologies is being carried out: If data should be used also for research purposes (for example in clinical settings in which many examinees with the same pathology are assessed), a fixed battery is desirable, in order to have complete and systematic data. If there is the need of better understanding some details of an already known cognitive deficit of an examinee, a flexible battery may be preferred.

4.7 The issue of multiple testing in neuropsychological assessment

When administering multiple tests during an assessment, the probability of error and of drawing wrong conclusions increases with the number of tests administered. There is always an inherent probability of error in test administration and this will be discussed in detail in Chapters 5 and 7. Here, it is sufficient to assume that when a score suggests a potential impairment, one cannot consider the result as 'true', but rather as indicating the probability of being wrong (typically, a very low probability). Importantly, the more tests are administered, the higher the chance that a conclusion is incorrect, depending on the specific statistical assumptions (e.g., a result below cut-off even though an examinee's performance is unimpaired, see Chapter 5).

This is related to the well-known issue of multiple comparisons (Benjamini & Hochberg, 1995; Benjamini & Yekutieli, 2001; Gelman, Hill, & Yajima, 2012). Many of the proposed correction methods to account for this effect are not applicable in the case of neuropsychological assessment because they would require knowledge of the exact probability associated with the observed performance and not only whether it is below/above cut-offs (Chapter 5 shows how techniques, such as z-scores, allow the calculation of the percentage of the normative sample that scored equal to or below the observed score).

An alternative approach to the correction for multiple comparisons in neuropsychology is based on the analysis of 'patterns' in neuropsychological test scores, rather than individual scores. This avoids the problem of multiple comparisons since the total scores are considered as a whole (Silverstein, 1982; Miller & Rohling, 2001). Unfortunately, very few test batteries used this method to determine the presence of impairments, and the neuropsychologist typically uses assessment tests where the ability to identify score patterns is not statistically defined.

The problem of multiple testing is particularly relevant in cases where a specific diagnosis is based on detecting a deficit in at least a certain number of tests. This is, for instance, the case of the diagnosis of cognitive impairment in Amyotrophic Lateral Sclerosis (ALS). According to the Consus criteria (Strong et al., 2017), ALS patients are classified as having cognitive deficit if they show deficient performance in at least two cognitive tests related to executive functions, from a given list of tests. This criterion is problematic because it does not specify exactly which and how many tests should be administered. It is obvious that the choice of tests can influence the results, but so can the number of tests. For example, an examinee who is given only three executive function tests is less likely to be classified as ALS with cognitive impairment than an examinee who is given ten executive function tests. In the second case we are more likely to find a deficit (even if the deficit is not really present), simply because more tests have been administered. In using these diagnostic criteria, it is therefore important to try to find the right balance, referring to more concrete examples in the literature for the choice of how many tests to administer.

In many cases, there is no easy way to properly take into account the issue of multiple testing in neuropsychological assessment, at least from a statistical perspective. A neuropsychologist should be aware that as the number of tests used increases, the probability of making errors increases too. This is partly in contrast to the frequent belief that a more accurate assessment is necessarily based on the administration of a large number of tests.

Notes

1. Here the term 'construct' denotes an unobservable psychological concept. In clinical neuropsychology, constructs are most often cognitive functions, but there are cases in which constructs represent other types of more general concepts (such as autonomy in daily life, status of executive functions, etc.).
2. These considerations are an extension of the concept of 'validity of performance' developed in the context of forensic neuropsychology, and refer to the process of evaluating whether results from tests are valid and reflect the

investigated cognitive functions, or whether they are invalid – for instance, if they are affected by motivation/effort (Greher & Wodushek, 2017).

3. For an in-depth study of Rasch's models see Bond & Fox (2007). Note that there are there are also further, more general definitions of measurement in science https://plato.stanford.edu/entries/measurement-science/#QuaMagBriHis. Based on some of them, it would not be appropriate to claim, say, that one measures an object, because what is measured are properties of objects.

5   Test scores

This chapter discusses how to use test scores in a neuropsychological assessment to detect cognitive impairments. In particular, the chapter will discuss two aspects: 1. normative data; and 2. thresholds for impairments, or normality cut-offs. The chapter also discusses how test scores can be used for other aims; for instance' to compare performance in different tests or to investigate changes over time, in order to measure improvements or declines.

The main role of tests in neuropsychological assessment is to assess cognitive performance, possibly identifying cognitive deficits.

Suppose an examinee is assessed following a head injury to assess whether they may have a short-term memory deficit. A valid test to measure short-term memory is administered (e.g., the Digit span) and the score obtained is 4. What does the score '4' indicate? Is this an indicator of a cognitive deficit, or not?

In order to draw this conclusion, the practice is to refer to some reference values, or a cut-off value, which is a threshold below which the performance is considered impaired, thus reflecting a cognitive impairment. This chapter focuses on the meaning of *normality cut-off*, on how it is calculated, and on the concepts that the neuropsychologist needs to know in order to properly use cut-offs. To calculate the *normality cut-off* of a test, it is necessary to use *normative data*, the main topic of the next paragraph.

5.1 Normative data

Normative data are the scores obtained from a reference sample of people whose performance is assumed to be unimpaired or 'normal'.[1] Normative data have several functions, the most important being to define a *normality cut-off* (or *cut-offs*), i.e., the threshold value below which a performance is considered to be impaired.

DOI: 10.4324/9781003195221-5

As the cut-off is typically a pointwise threshold, an observed performance that corresponds to the cut-off (e.g., an observed score of 5, when the cut-off score is 5), is sometimes considered a *borderline* score, to underline the uncertainty of the observed performance.[2]

In some cases, more than one threshold is available, but these are often simple extensions of cases with just one threshold.

Although it is fairly straightforward to use the normality cut-offs that are provided with a test, it is important to clarify all the implicit assumptions made when using normative data and cut-offs, and the rationale for their use.

5.1.1 The rationale for using normative data

When assessing an examinee with a suspected cognitive impairment, the aim is to understand whether such cognitive deficit is present following a specific event (e.g., a stroke, a head injury, a neurosurgical operation) or whether instead the deficit signals the onset of a neurodegenerative disease (e.g., of Alzheimer's disease).

Ideally, it would be critical to know the examinee's test score *before* the lesion/deterioration, and to be able to compare the original performance with the current performance. Unfortunately, this is a very rare occurrence, and very often no information is available. A potential solution to these missing data is to estimate the expected score from this examinee if unimpaired. To make this estimate, we use the scores of other people without cognitive impairment – i.e., 'normal' – who are *similar* to the examinee we need to evaluate. In clinical neuropsychology, 'similar' refers to factors known to most influence performance on cognitive deficits, usually age, education, and in some cases gender (Strauss et al., 2006; Spinnler & Tognoni, 1987). To summarise, starting from a group of people assumed to be similar to the examinee and assumed to have no cognitive impairment, we can estimate the expected score for that examinee. If the examinee's score is worse than what is expected from an estimate of their expected score (made from similar people), then we conclude that the individual is likely to have a cognitive impairment.

Testing participants who are similar to the examinee is a resource-intensive task, and for this reason, most neuropsychological tests already provide normative data, i.e., summary information from a large group of healthy people. Such normative data can be used as a reference to compare the scores that are assessed by the clinician with that test. The test instructions usually already explain how to use these normative data in order to compare them in a way that is appropriate to the examinee's performance.

Since the concepts discussed in this paragraph are extremely important for the correct use of normality cut-offs, they will be reinforced using a concrete example. Let's go back to the examinee mentioned at the beginning of the chapter. This individual was given a valid test to measure short-term memory (the Digit Span) and the score obtained was equal to 4. Let us assume that this examinee is 35 years old and has a high school education (i.e., 13 years of education) and let us assume that we are using some normative data provided with the ENB-2 (Mondini et al., 2011) for the Digit Span test. To understand whether a score of 4 may indicate an impaired performance, we compare it with that from people who are similar to our examinee, in this case with people who have similar age and education, and that we assume have no cognitive impairment in short-term memory. The ENB-2 tables indicate that the normality cut-off for the Digit Span test, for the combination of 35 years of age and more than 8 years of education, is 5. This indicates that a score below 5 should be considered as potentially indicating impaired performance (see Chapter 6 for interpretation of test scores). The score of 4 obtained by the examinee now becomes meaningful, and indicates that the examinee is likely to have a cognitive deficit following the head injury. Note that in concluding that there is a deficit there is an (implicit) assumption that the examinee's condition worsened, namely that they changed with respect to a previous condition (in this specific case worsening followed the head trauma). If we (hypothetically) knew with certainty that the examinee scored 4 even before the head trauma, the information of being 'impaired', i.e., below the cut-off, would have had completely different implications and interpretations. This issue will be further discussed in the section on test interpretation (see Chapter 6).

Some tests try to explicitly estimate the expected premorbid abilities, and can be directly used on an examinee. One such test is the National Adult Reading Test (NART, Nelson, 1982) which is based on the assumption that reading abilities are often resistent to brain damage. This is however a different way to estimate an examinee's premorbid cognitive abilities, as it is based on inferring them from their performance on a test rather than from a comparison with a normative sample.

For sake of clarity, we make a precise distinction here between 'neuropsychological assessment' – which evaluates a potential pathological condition (e.g., neurological) which may have affected cognitive functioning – and 'cognitive assessment' – which evaluates the cognitive functioning of an examinee who has not suffered from a known neurological/pathological event, for instance to assess their fitness to drive, for sport-related assessments, or by human resources. In the case of cognitive assessment, a performance below normality cut-off may be relevant from a clinical point of view even if it may not reflect a decline. This is for example the case of developmental disorders which are not the result of a known neurological/pathological event but reflect a pre-existing condition.

To conclude, it is important to emphasise that there are two implicit assumptions in the use of normative data that are often overlooked or ignored:

1 Normative data are used to estimate expected performance of an examinee with reference to data of people assumed to have no cognitive impairment and who are similar to the examinee.
2 In the neuropsychological assessment, the fact that a performance score refers to an impaired or normal level is not in itself relevant, but is important to make inferences about an examinee's cognitive state getting worse with respect to an event (e.g., a stroke, a degeneration related to Alzheimer's disease, etc.).

5.2 Collection of normative data

Normative data allow us to refer to what has been defined as the normality cut-off and thus to detect a cognitive impairment. To understand the meaning of the normality cut-off, it is useful to understand how the collection of normative data takes place.

Let's suppose there is an ongoing normative data collection, for a test whose scores range from 0 to 7. Without reference, we don't know if a score of 0 or 1 or 2, or 6 or 7, can indicate something important about a participant's performance and helps us in the neuropsychological assessment. For example, the test could be very difficult so even obtaining 2 or 3 could be considered a good performance. On the contrary (and this is typically what happens with neuropsychological tests), the test could be very easy, and even a performance with relatively high scores (e.g., 6 or 7 out of 10) could be somewhat unexpected from a healthy person, and thus the signal of a potential cognitive impairment. To make this kind of inferences we need to know the distribution of scores of a reference group (typically, healthy people without cognitive impairment) on that test, which is considered to be 'normal'. Hence the name 'normative' data.

In this hypothetical normative data collection, the first participant scored '5' (See Figure 5.1, panel a). The x-axis indicates the scores

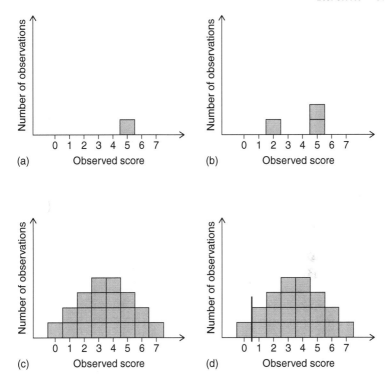

Figure 5.1

obtained in the test, the y-axis reports the number of participants who obtained that score. Let's assume that two other participants scored '2' and '5' respectively (see Figure 5.1, panel b). Figure 5.1, panel c represents a possible distribution for 20 observations. Once this empirical distribution of scores has been obtained, after making a number of assumptions, it is possible to calculate the score that referring to specific portions of the distribution. In particular, this refers to specific percentages of observations (5%, 10%, 20% etc.). A particularly important value is the one delimiting the 5% of the worst scores. Assuming that in our test lower scores correspond to worse performance, 5% of the worst scores will be on the left of our distribution (see Figure 5.1, panel d). We define this threshold as *normality cut-off*: if an examinee obtains a score below this value, then their performance is considered impaired (or pathological).

Scores equal to or above this value are considered to be normal (i.e., not impaired). Note that the term 'clinical' cut-off, has been deliberately avoided to avoid confusion: the threshold in itself does not necessarily imply a clinical meaning (a clinical meaning is, rather, an interpretation of the score, see Chapter 6).

Choosing just 5% is an arbitrary convention, dominant in the psychological and social sciences, whereby an alpha of 0.05 is considered the threshold for a statistically significant result. In some cases, thresholds provided with the test use different percentages (e.g., Delazer et al., 2003 in a battery for numbers and calculation used 10%).

Within the normative sample (i.e., of participants whom we have assumed to be normal), there will always be some normal participants who have obtained a value below the cut-off. For example, in Figure 5.1, panel d the small square to the left of the black bar represents the performance of a normal subject who obtained a score below what it is defined as the normality cut-off. It is important to remember that a value below the cut-off is only suggestive – based on statistical properties – rather than conclusive on the presence of a cognitive impairment. This aspect will be discussed in more detail in the next section.

5.3 The meaning of cut-offs

So far, we discussed how a score below the cut-off may indicate an impaired performance, specifically getting worse. A conclusion that performance below the cut-off is impaired is made on a probabilistic basis: we cannot be certain that the performance is actually impaired and that damage has actually occurred, but the cut-off helps us to draw this conclusion. Since only a few participants similar to the examinee (and without cognitive impairment) performed so low, we conclude that the score observed is likely a symptom of cognitive impairment.

But what is the probability that the observed performance is actually below the cut-off of normality?

Let's go back to our example and imagine that we have observed performance to be below the cut-off (i.e., 5% of scores worse than the normative data). A common mistake is to conclude that with a value below the cut-off there is a probability smaller than 5% that the assessed individual is *normal*. In fact, the cut-off indicates that, assuming the individual is normal, there is less than a 5% chance of observing a score equal or lower than the observed one. When tests that provide normative data are used, all that can be established is how unlikely it is to observe this performance if we assume the examinee is unimpaired.

This kind of reasoning (somewhat counter-intuitive) is the same used in statistics when adopting the frequentist approach and the p-values. A p-value of less than 0.05 corresponds to a statistically significant result and involves accepting the alternative hypothesis. However, when obtaining a p-value below 0.05, we do not really make specific statements about the alternative hypothesis, but we accept it only because if we assume that the null hypothesis is true, there is a probability of less than 5% (p < 0.05) of observing the results that are actually obtained. In the same way when we use a normality cut-off, we conclude that an individual has a cognitive deficit (analogue of the alternative hypothesis) because if we assume that he is an unimpaired participant (analogue of the null hypothesis) it would be extremely unlikely to observe the score that we have actually observed. The importance of the precise meaning of the cut-offs will become clearer later in the chapter and will be further expanded in Chapter 7.

5.4 The most common methods for calculating normality cut-offs

There are numerous methods for calculating cut-offs, some mathematically quite complex (e.g., Crawford & Garthwaite, 2006; Crawford et al., 2010).

Knowing the simpler methods of calculating cut-offs can clarify their meaning and some of the misuses. One of the most common methods of calculating cut-offs is based on the transformation of scores into z-scores (Strauss et al., 2006). From a mathematical point of view, the z-score transformation (also known as standardisation) converts a set of scores (in our case the scores from normative data collection) into scores that have mean 0 and standard deviation 1. The formula for calculating z-scores is as follows:

$$z\text{-}score = \frac{(raw\ score\ of\ the\ examinee) - (mean\ of\ reference\ group)}{(standard\ deviation\ of\ the\ reference\ group)}$$

If the distribution of the data is approximately normal/Gaussian (like the one in Figure 5.1 panel d) the z-scores can be used to bound some percentages of the distribution. In particular, the value $z = -1.64$ delimits 5% for lower scores and is often used as a normality cut-off. The use of z-scores (when possible) is very handy: it is sufficient to know the mean and standard deviation of the normative reference data and apply the formula to know the normality cut-off. Also, as any z-score (under some assumption) corresponds to specific percentages, we can know the exact probability associated with an observed performance. Suppose for instance we have a test with mean = 50 and SD = 8. The examinee we assessed scored 35. Standardising (i.e., transforming to a z-score) the score, $z = (35-50)/8 = -1.875$. Since the score is less than $z = -1.64$ the value is below the cut-off of 5% of the worst scores and therefore allows us to say that the performance is below the norm. The use of z-scores has the additional advantage of allowing us to define exactly what percentage of the data delimits the value obtained by the subject. Using a statistical program or checking the z-score distribution tables, it can be seen that -1.875 delimits 3.07% of the score distribution (on the web, it is easy to find z-score to percentage converters, and formulas for this transformation).

A further advantage of z-scores is that they allow comparison of scores obtained in different tests by the same examinee (see the end of this chapter).

However, an important implicit assumption made when using z-scores is that the distribution of the data is normal/Gaussian. The correspondence of specific z-scores to known percentages of the data is only valid if the distribution of the data is approximately normal/Gaussian. If the distribution has a different shape, the relationship may change. For example, the value -1.64 may not define the worst 5% of data, so relying on this value may be inappropriate for calculating cut-offs (assuming that we want to consider the 5% of worst scores as the cut-off). Consider the distribution of normative data shown in Figure 5.2 is not actually normal/Gaussian (it is not symmetrical and it has a longer tail on the left). The observed distribution of scores is due to the more common characteristic of neuropsychological tests,

Normal Distribution   **Non-normal Distribution**

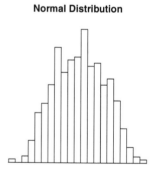 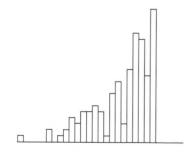

Figure 5.2

i.e., to be rather simple for healthy participants, who tend to obtain high scores. With such characteristics, the score tends to show the so-called 'ceiling' effect, which is associated with non-normal data distribution.

If the score distribution is not normal, there are other methods to calculate normality cut-offs. One is to rely on non-parametric percentiles method (see for example, Delazer et al., 2003). Non-parametric methods, differently from parametric methods (including the use of z-scores), can be used independently of the shape of the data distribution. However, using non-parametric percentiles has the disadvantage that it is not possible to calculate the percentage a specific observed score corresponds to, as it has been explained for z-score. For example, suppose a 20 years old examinee obtained a score of 15 in the Addition Task of the Number and Calculations Test Battery (NPC) by Delazer and colleagues (2003). This observed performance is below the cut-off score of 18 reported in the normative data table. Since the cut-offs are calculated with non-parametric percentiles, it is not possible to know exactly the percentage of data delimited by the observed performance (i.e., 15). Despite this drawback, if the score distribution of a test is not gaussian, especially with strongly skewed data or multimodal distributions, it is more appropriate to use non-parametric percentiles rather than z-scores, to avoid incorrect conclusions.

All of the methods discussed in this section, the parametric and non-parametric, make an implicit assumption, namely that they treat normative data as population data rather than sample data. The distinction between sample and population is the subject of the next section.

5.5 The difference between sample and population in the use of normative data.

Figure 5.1 (panel d), shows the results of a hypothetical normative data collection. The group of participants on which the data is collected is called the *normative sample*. The concept of 'sample' is very important in statistics and, as a consequence, also in clinical neuropsychology. It is closely linked to the concept of population. In particular, the normative sample is a group of participants extracted from a larger population of participants.

To understand the difference between these two concepts and the impact on the use of normality cut-offs, it is useful to consider a practical example. Suppose we have collected normative data for a group of participants aged 30 to 40 years with education higher than 15 years.

Our normative data consist of a number of participants, for example 50. Let us assume that the normality cut-off (calculated using non-parametric percentiles) is 7. This result indicates that in these 50 participants only 5% (so about three people) scored below 7. The problem with this normality cut-off is that it is contextual to the 50 participants included in the data collection. If data were to be collected on other 50 participants, we cannot be sure the normality cut-off would be again the score 7. The 50 participants on whom the cut-off was calculated constitute a *sample* (i.e., a subset) of the population, which is made up of all possible participants aged between 30 and 40 years and with education of more than 15 years. The crucial aspect of this distinction is that the interest is never in the sample itself (to refer to our example, the interest is not on the performance of those specific 50 participants), but on the population from which the sample is drawn (i.e., in all possible participants with the characteristics of being aged between 30 and 40 and having education of more than 15 years). Remember that the purpose of using normative data is to estimate the performance we should expect from an examinee. Our estimate would be more accurate if we could use the whole population, i.e., all possible participants with similar characteristics to the individual we want to assess, than if we could only consider 50 participants. Obviously, for practical reasons, this is not possible: we cannot obtain data on the whole population, and we only collect data on smaller samples. The larger the sample, the more likely that it is representative of the population from which it is drawn, which is why normative samples often have hundreds of participants.

To account for the distinction between sample and population, several statistical methods have been proposed which basically try to control for the imprecision associated with using a subset of the population. To be more specific, methods that take into account the sample/population distinction tend to provide lower cut-offs (thus being more conservative in defining the threshold for impairment). In general, the smaller the sample size, the more conservative the cut-off, i.e., the lower it is. Going back to the above example, in our sample of 50 participants the cut-off obtained was 7. Applying a method that takes into account the sample/population distinction, the resulting normality cut-off may be 6. If the cut-off of 7 had been obtained from a smaller sample (e.g., 20 subjects) the estimated cut-off for the population could instead be 4 (thus even more conservative). This is due to the fact that the smaller the sample, the less precise we are in estimating the population cut-off and the more likely it is that the observed cut-off depends on some anomaly in the collected sample, rather than a systematic aspect reflecting the population property.

There are some very rigorous methods that take into account the distinction between sample and population, such as those proposed by John Crawford (Crawford & Howell, 1998; Crawford & Garthwaite, 2006; and all methods developed by John Crawford, see https://homepages. abdn.ac.uk/j.crawford/pages/dept/SingleCaseMethodology.htm).

The method of the Equivalent Scores is another which takes into account this distinction (Capitani & Laiacona, 1999). This method has a parametric component, i.e., the calculation of a multiple regression (see section 5.6) and a non-parametric component, i.e., the calculation of tolerance limits, which takes into account the difference between sample and population. Tests using methods that take into account the sample/population distinction should be considered methodologically more rigorous than the use of simple non-parametric percentiles or z-score calculated on the sample.

5.6 Fundamental aspects of normative data

The use of normative data represents a very important part of the clinical activity of a neuropsychologist. Often the neuropsychologist, after choosing which test to use based on its validity, also needs to choose which normative data to refer to. The choice of different normative data can lead to different conclusions, since the normality cut-offs may be quite different in different data collections. In the following paragraphs, the key features of using and choosing normative data will be discussed. The link between all these sections is the fact that, in order to be used properly, normative data must be representative, i.e., made up of participants similar to the examinee.

5.6.1 Considering demographic variables in normative data

This chapter focuses on how to compare an examinee's score with normative data in order to understand whether their performance is unexpected and likely to be the sign of a cognitive deficit. In an ideal situation, the examinee's score is compared with their own score prior to the onset of the neurological disorder (e.g., Alzheimer's) or the damaging event that led to the cognitive deficit (e.g., a stroke or a head injury). *In such a case, a comparison with normative data is unnecessary, as there is an actual reference to the performance of the very same participant to examine whether there has been a change.*

However, since this is rarely possible, the score obtained by an examinee is typically compared with those obtained by a control group (which comes from the normative data), namely with a group of participants similar to the examinee. To define this control group, three main variables are usually taken into account: age, education, and sex (Slick, 2006b). These are sometimes called generically as 'demographic variables', as they are the main demographic aspects that are known to be associated with performance, which can be easily and quickly collected during the assessment. The effect of age and education on performance on cognitive tests is a well-known phenomenon in the literature and in almost all studies of experimental cognitive neuropsychology (but also of cognitive psychology) in which an experimental group is compared with a control group. The situation is similar in a neuropsychological assessment, where instead of experimental groups we have an examinee, and instead of the control group we have the participant composing the normative data.

Many neuropsychological tests tend to show worse performance with increasing age and better performance with higher education. This is, however, a simplification and reflects only a general trend and in some tests (e.g., some related to specific verbal skills) performance may improve with age (Slick, 2006b). Furthermore, several tests may show non-linear relationships with plateaus (see for example Arcara & Bambini, 2016; Arcara et al., 2017; Cherner et al., 2021). Some tests also take into account other demographic variables of the subject, the type of work (manual/high intellectual demand), or even estimates of the Cognitive Reserve (Montemurro et al., 2022). Although the discussion will mainly focus on the main variables of age, education, and sex, this can be extended to any variable that is considered relevant for the normative data.

To account for differences in demographic variables, tables are provided to stratify the normative data according to these variables such that it is possible to compare an examinee with a subset of matched normative data. Other tests instead use correction methods based on more complex mathematical formulas (e.g., regression). These allow establishing whether the examinee's performance is impaired on the basis of a comparison of the observed scores with those predicted from the age and education values (e.g., Angeleri et al., 2012). These formulas are most often linked to multiple linear or non-linear regressions.

Sometimes these tests provide methods to adjust for variables such as age, education and sex, generally resulting in a single normality cut-off. Before comparing with this single cut-off, it is necessary to adjust the score of the examinee on the basis of their age, education, and sex (by applying appropriate formulas). These adjusting methods tend to compensate for the expected performance of the examinees based on their demographic features. For instance, if high scores are expected (e.g., from young and/or highly educated examinees), the observed scores are lowered, and if low scores are expected (e.g., from older or poorly educated examinees), the observed scores may be increased.

There are two main advantages in using correction methods based on regressions instead of stratification methods (e.g., Santangelo et al., 2015), or those separating age and education groups (e.g., Ouvrard et al., 2019). The first is that after the 'correction' for demographic variables, all participants can be considered as equal and thus a single (and large) normative sample is created from which the cut-off can be calculated. With a single large sample, the cut-off more closely reflects the cut-off of the whole population, while cut-offs of several smaller samples tend to be less accurate.

The second advantage of 'correction' methods is that they avoid abrupt steps when moving from one age group or education to another. Consider for example, an hypothetical individual with 50 years of age and no diploma who performs the Trail Making Test B (Reitan, 1958). For this example we will refer to the Ouvrard et al. (2019) cut-off tables, which are based on discrete separation into age bins. In this test, the score is represented by the number of seconds required to complete the task: the higher the score, the worse the performance. According to the tables provided, the cut-off for this participant is 40 seconds: a performance with a score higher than 40 is to be considered impaired (if we assume that the cut-off is that delimiting 5% of worse scores). If, however, our subject had been 52 years old (i.e., only two years older) the cut-off would be 45, i.e., 5 seconds higher. The division into discrete groups, in this case, has created a relatively large 'step' in the cut-offs. In this case a reasonable solution is to take into account this aspect in the interpretation of the cut-off and, for example, to consider both the cut-offs in interpretations (see Chapter 7, where this specific example is discussed again).

Regression-based correction methods, on the other hand, do not suffer from this problem of abrupt cut-off changes. However, it has long been known in the literature (Fastenau, 1998; O'Connell et al., 2011) that regression-based adjustment methods have other issues. In particular, in certain cases they can lead to a distorted estimate of the examinee's performance and therefore to an inappropriate use of the normality cut-offs. It is beyond the scope of this book to go into this in depth (see in particular the article by Fastenau, 1998). In particular, and following well-known properties of linear regressions, one should be careful about scores that have extreme values in the demographic variables (very high or very low education or age). Due to properties of regressions, indeed, these scores are those that might suffer more from distortions in the calculations of cut-offs.

To summarise, there are two main methods for taking into account the effects of demographic variables on test performance: separate tables dividing in bins, or adjustments by regressions. Although these methods are different, they serve the same purpose: to compare an individual's score with a normality cut-off in such a way that the performance of control subjects (normative data) as similar as possible to him or her is taken into account.

5.6.2 Normative data from very large groups are not necessarily better

There is often a widespread belief that normative data from very large groups are better than normative data from small groups of subjects. This claim is partly correct and related to the considerations made earlier, about the difference between sample and population: the larger a reference sample is, the more likely it is that the values we calculate of the normality cut-offs will be close to those that would be obtained for the whole population. However, estimating an examinee's performance depends on the size of the sample of the normative data, on its characteristics and how close these are to the examinee.

For example, suppose we have to assess, after a traumatic brain injury, an English female examinee with 20 years of age and a high school diploma. Suppose we use a test in which the normative data have been collected on a sample of 1500 persons, therefore with a large numerosity. Let us assume that for this test the normative data are divided into bands and that the group of interest (age 20–25 and education is High School diploma) includes 30 subjects. However, let's assume that, a better inspection of the normative data reveals that in this age bin, most of people had an age of 24 and 25 and only two participants had an age of 20. This would indicate that (no matter the size of the normative sample) we have little data that can help us in defining the expected performance for our examinee.

Note that the adequacy (or better, the inadequacy) of our comparison, would be independent of the method used to calculate the cut-offs (divided into bands or with regression-based corrections): if there are no (or few) participants in the normative data that adequately reflect the individual to be assessed, then our estimation of his or her performance and thus the comparison with the cut-off will be hard to interpret.

It is always important to understand that for a meaningful use of normative data our examinee must be adequately represented. There are many other cases in which we may believe that our normative data are inappropriate. This could be for people with a life history that could not be represented in the normative data sample. For example: an individual with no formal education, but an intensive house-education, a migrant who moved at a specific age in the country in which is assessed, an individual with a peculiar history of education achievements (e.g., more than one degree, winner of prizes on his branch), and so on.

The examples given above refer to very specific cases of people who is likely to be under-represented in any test on the normative data, but this reasoning can be extended to less extreme situations. Indeed, it could be the case that, due to feasibility constraints, the normative data of a specific test can show underrepresentation of a specific combination of demographic variables.

In such cases, rather than relying on such normative data it might be better to rely on a relatively small sample of people collected ad-hoc (e.g., ten participants), but who have similar characteristics to the individual to be assessed, i.e., female with about 20 years of age and a high school diploma. For this purpose, on the website of John R. Crawford, several free softwares are available which allow the calculation of cut-offs for small groups of normative data, also consisting of 5-10 healthy participants (https://homepages.abdn.ac.uk/j.crawford/pages/dept/SingleCaseMethodsComputerPrograms.HTM).

5.6.3 The importance of using up-to-date normative data

Another very important aspect of using normative data is related to how recently they have been collected. James R. Flynn, was the first to note in 1987 that the average IQ of people seems to increase over the generations (Flynn, 1987). The explanation for the Flynn effect has been traced back to sociocultural changes that have led to an increase in abstract logic skills, which are crucial in IQ tests (Williams, 2013). Of extreme relevance is the fact that the Flynn effect is also observed in neuropsychological tests and not only in IQ tests (Hiscock, 2007). Interestingly, recent studies have evidenced a Negative Flynn effect, that is a change in the trend and a decrease of performance in IQ test over time (Dutton et al., 2016) in many countries. There have been some tentative explanations of this trend inversion, suggesting that it may be related to environmental factors (Bratsberg & Rogeberg, 2018). Despite the potential explanations, the Flynn effect (and the negative Flynn effect), have a relevant practical consequence: it is important to use up-to-date normative data. Normative data obtained almost 30 years ago may no longer be adequate to estimate the cognitive test performance of examinees assessed today. All things being equal, it would therefore be better to always use the most up-to-date normative data possible. If the normative data are old, then they should be used with extreme caution and this aspect should be taken into account in the interpretation.

5.6.4 The importance of using country-specific standards

A common (and deeply flawed) practice sometimes used in clinical neuropsychology is to adapt a neuropsychological test from a language to another by a simple translation of the items. A translated test should undergo further studies to confirm its validity, as the translation of items may alter the already known properties (see section 4.2). An additional and crucial problem lies in the use of normative data collected in different countries, even if the test does not need a translation. In particular, even if the age and education of the normative sample are comparable and even if language is the same, this is not sufficient to make it possible to use the normative data for people of another country. There are in fact other socio-cultural variables which can have an important influence on test performance. The influence of such variables is well known in the United States of America where normative data are often also divided by ethnic group (with consequent controversies, Slick, 2006b).

A striking case on the problems of using inappropriate normative data from other countries is related to the initial use of MoCA (Nasreddine et al., 2005) in Italy. Initially developed for the Canadian population, the translation of the MoCA has been available in Italy for several years (Pirani et al., 2006), and following its translation, the MoCA immediately became very popular and widespread in clinical settings. After a short time, however, it was clear enough (and informally discussed in conferences or across specialists) that the Canadian cut-off was absolutely inadequate in Italy, since most elderly subjects obtain lower scores. The normative data published in Italy on the MoCA are only more recent than its initial diffusion (Arcara et al., 2013; Pirrotta et al., 2014; Conti et al., 2015, Santangelo et al., 2014; Montemurro et al., 2022). Similar differences were noted in other adaptations of MoCA. For example, in the German adaptation of Thomann and colleagues (2018), 31% of the normative sample scored below the original cut-off of the Canadian version.

There are numerous reasons why tests calibrated in one country may not be adequate in another country: due to sociocultural differences, economic differences, language-related differences, education methods, or familiarity with taking structured tests, etc. Regardless of the reason for these differences, it is important to consider that normative data obtained with people who are too different from the one we want to assess (and people from a different country certainly are) may not be representative and their use may lead to radically wrong conclusions.

5.7 Other uses of tests

5.7.1 *Assessing change over time using neuropsychological tests*

A very common need in clinical neuropsychology is to monitor change in cognitive status over time. This may be necessary for several reasons:

- To investigate whether an examinee has changed after a rehabilitation treatment.
- To investigate whether an examinee shows a decline in cognitive functioning, as possibly a sign of progressive degeneration.
- To investigate whether an examinee has undergone cognitive changes following an event that can be predicted, such as a neurosurgical operation to remove a brain tumour.

In these cases we have two (or more) measurements at different times and the aim is to find out if a significant change has occurred. Suppose an examinee scored 24 on the MMSE (Folstein, Folstein, & McHugh, 1975) and after three months scored 22. Should this discrepancy be considered a significant change? Or can it be traced back to a natural fluctuation of the score related to the properties of the test?

A first fundamental aspect to consider in these cases is that for no neuropsychological test is it expected that the measurement will be exactly the same between two measurements, even if nothing has changed in what is measured. This aspect is captured (partly) by test-retest reliability, a value that expresses the consistency of two measurements (see section 4.2). Tests with low test-retest reliability have spontaneous random fluctuations in the score and should not be used to monitor changes over time. Having high test-retest reliability is, however, a necessary but not sufficient condition for using a test to assess change: test-retest reliability is a quality that captures the influence of random oscillations between two measurements, but not of systematic ones.

Systematic effects between two neuropsychological test measurements are effects that are expected to be shown by all subjects to whom the test is administered, in a similar way.

The most common systematic effect observed between two measurements with a neuropsychological test is the 'practice effect' (McCaffrey & Westervelt, 1995). The practice effect refers to a systematic improvement that is observed in participants when they repeat a test. There are several reasons for this effect: a person who takes a test for the second time is usually less anxious, is more familiar with the test situation and the examiner and may already have a strategy in mind for dealing with the task more efficiently.

Another effect that may influence the estimate of change is the 'regression to the mean' (Salinsky et al., 2001). This effect refers to the fact that, in general, if a person has achieved an extremely high or low performance in a first assessment, it is expected that they will be closer to the average at a second assessment, i.e., achieve a less extreme performance. This is because, from a statistical point of view, exceptionally high or low performance is probably due, at least in part, to random events that occurred during the measurement (perhaps the individual was particularly fatigued or was very lucky in answering some items) and it is likely that these random events will no longer be present in a further measurement.

All these considerations highlight the problematic nature of the common practice of simply relying on a comparison between two tests to conclude that a change has occurred. The influence of random fluctuations or systematic effects means that two measurements on the same individual rarely lead to the same result. Hence, it becomes fundamental for a neuropsychologist to understand when a certain discrepancy can be considered the effect of a real change.

In order to be able to answer this question appropriately, there are specially developed statistical methods that take fluctuations (systematic and random) into account and provide threshold values above which a change is considered to be significant (Jacobson & Truax, 1991; Collie et al., 2011; Crawford & Garthwaite, 2006). This is done by collecting data from two measurements, separated in time, in a group in which no difference in the measured construct is expected. Any variation observed between the two measurements is assumed to be attributable to test properties, random fluctuations or systematic effects, but not to changes in the underlying cognitive function. From this data (which will have a similar function to normative data) it is therefore possible to compare data on the change in an individual, e.g., an examinee following rehabilitation. If the observed score at the second measurement shows a change that is not expected from the normal fluctuations estimated from the control group, it is inferred that a significant change has occurred.

In the American context it is common for tests to provide statistical methods for assessing change over time (Strauss et al., 2006) but the same does not seem to be the case in other countries, like in Italy (Barletta-Rodolfi, Gasparini, & Ghidoni, 2011; Aiello et al., 2021).

A clinical neuropsychologist often needs to assess change with a test that does not include appropriate methodology for this type of inference (e.g., tables or thresholds for significant changes). In this case the clinician should prefer to use a test with high test-retest reliability, evidence of low practice effect, and following the rationale of this book, taking into account the lack of precise evidence in interpreting the results. In general, as an obvious rule-of-thumb, small changes in absence of empirical data on thresholds of significant change, should be interpreted with extreme caution. Finally, clinical neuropsychologist can also make up for these shortcomings by their own by using some freely available sources on the internet (see again the website of Prof. John R. Crawford, http://homepages.abdn.ac.uk/j.crawford/pages/dept/psychom.htm), and collecting small samples to determine thresholds for significant change.

5.7.2 Comparing the results of different neuropsychological tests

In some cases it may be useful to compare results from different neuropsychological tests. For example, it might be relevant to know whether the examinee has a deficit in short-term memory that is much greater than the deficit in spatial attention, or the neuropsychologist might want to compare the result on different tests that measure the same cognitive function, to see whether they give similar results.

Scores on different tests, and especially tests measuring different cognitive functions, are in themselves incommensurable and cannot be compared. This is obvious when one considers that tests use different score ranges.

The most common strategy used in neuropsychology to allow these types of comparisons is to refer to normative data, and to the percentage of people who had similar (or lower) performance. This conversion is obtained from normative data and the procedure is exactly the same as that used to obtain normality cut-offs. It is possible, indeed, to convert each score with a percentage of the participant in the control group, who obtained a score equal to or lower than the one observed (e.g., 10%, 20%, 30% etc.). With this conversion it can be assumed that a score is converted into a sort of 'level' in the cognitive function measured.

For example, suppose we have an examinee who scores a 3 (on a scale of 0 to 6) on a short-term memory test and a score of 10 (on a scale of 0 to 20) on an abstraction test. Suppose that a score of 3 on the short-term memory test delimits 30% of the lowest performance (i.e., 30% of the subjects in the normative data scored 3 or lower) and a score of 10 delimits 70% of the lowest scores. This conversion suggests that performance is better on the abstraction test than on the short-term memory test.

Methods for making this conversion can be z-scores, non-parametric percentiles, or the use of equivalent scores (Capitani & Laiacona, 1997). Note that conversion using non-parametric percentiles and equivalent scores is only possible if these values have already been provided with the test. For a conversion with z-scores it is sufficient to have mean and standard deviation of the test, but to be meaningful, the test scores should have approximately a Gaussian distribution. In the case of conversion of scores to allow for comparison between different tests, the considerations made above about the sample/population for normative data still holds, and methods that refer to the population (such as Equivalent Scores) should be considered better than the others.

Notes

1. 'Normative data' refers to concepts different from normality (the content of this note is largely inspired by Capitani, 1997).

   The first meaning of normality is related to normative data. As mentioned, normative data refer to the scores obtained in a group of 'normal' participants. In this case the adjective 'normal' refers to individuals who are autonomous in their daily life and free from important pathologies that can influence performance in cognitive tasks. Thus, the group of participants included in the collection of normative data is assumed to be normal, often on the basis of characteristics of their functioning in daily life.

   The second meaning of 'normality' is related to the result of a neuropsychological test. It is usually concluded that a score is 'deficient' if it is below the cut-off or 'normal' if it is above the cut-off. In this case, whether the performance is 'in the normal range' or 'normal' is determined by comparing the score with normative data, and to a threshold score. So, while in the first meaning of 'normality' (the participants who compose the normative data are normal) 'normality' is a presupposition or an assumption, in this second meaning of 'normality' (the performance is normal because it is above the cut-off), being normal is rather a conclusion.

   Finally, a third meaning of normality is purely statistical and refers to a particular form of data distribution, the 'normal' distribution. In this case, normality refers to mathematical properties of the distribution, and not to qualities in the broad sense of being healthy, or not impaired (Capitani &

Laiacona, 2007). A neuropsychologist should be aware of this ambiguity and be careful in using the term 'normality', as it may refer to different meanings.
2. Some methods to calculate normality cut-off may include a range of scores that denote a 'grey area' of borderline performances between normality and impairment (e.g., Capitani & Laiacona, 1997).

6   Test scores: attribution and interpretation

This chapter describes two crucial phases in the use of a neuropsychological test: score attribution (or scoring) and test interpretation. The first phase highlights the active role of the neuropsychologist in attributing test scores, whenever the scores are not automatically attributed by a software or hardware (so, in most of paper-and-pencil tests). The second phase describes in detail one of the core assumptions of the framework put forward in the textbook, which conceptualises test interpretation as an active process that involves neuropsychologists and their prior knowledge in drawing any inference from tests. This process is characterised by the integration of all the information collected during the neuropsychological assessment, from the anamnesis and the interview to the neuropsychological test scores.

6.1 Test scoring

A crucial part of the use of tests is scoring. In the case of digital or self-administered neuropsychological tests, test scoring is automatically provided by the software, and scoring is not a complicated issue.

However, most of the tests used in clinical practice nowadays are paper-and-pencil tests, in which the score is assigned by the neuropsychologist. In the remainder of this section the focus will be on these traditional neuropsychological tests, in which scoring is an issue that deserves some consideration and reflection.

For each test (in its manual or reference published article), how to assign scores is always indicated. Before using a test, it is very important for the examiner to carefully learn the scoring method to check whether there are any peculiarities in scoring in specific situations. Tests in which the instructions are clear and the possible answers are precisely described (with follow-up explanation of how to assign scores) are much preferable to tests in which the attribution of scores is vague,

DOI: 10.4324/9781003195221-6

unclear or ambiguous. Tests with poorly detailed instructions are likely to have low inter-rater reliability (see section 4.2) and may give biassed estimates, since different examinees may attribute different scores to the same performance. Even if a test has high inter-rater reliability, and regardless of how detailed the instructions may be, there are cases where the scoring may be unclear.

A classic example of uncertain scoring is when there is a self-correction by the examinee following a wrong answer. Suppose, for example, that an examinee is taking a test, gives a wrong answer and corrects himself after an initial hesitation. How should this answer be considered? By treating it as wrong, one would overlook the fact that the person managed to get the correct answer. On the other hand, if one were to regard it as right, it would be regarded as identical to that of a person who immediately answered correctly and this, too, would be a questionable choice. Many tests do not specify what to do in such cases. It is important to note that, from a theoretical point of view, there is no 'ideal' and best approach to choosing how to score in ambiguous situations: the correct choice depends on how the data were collected during the development of the test.

If, therefore, there is an ambiguous case during the test scoring that is not covered by the test instructions, the examiner should take this into account and consider how much the item(s) with dubious attribution actually influence the final score and the conclusions drawn from the test. If ambiguity tends to occur frequently, the examiner may wish to contact the test developer directly and ask for clarification of the procedure used in developing the test.

Some specific styles and approaches during test administration and scoring can have an important influence on the final results. For example, a fairly common practice among some clinicians is to tend to encourage the examinee and to maximise the performance by making think about whether he/she gives wrong impulsive answers (e.g., asking after a mistake "are you sure about this answer?") and supporting the examinee through the test. A correct answer after encouragement is then considered correct in the scoring process. This very empathetic approach could be fundamentally flawed. During the development phase of the tests (and e.g., the calculation of cut-offs) it is plausible that a very formal, structured, and strict procedure was used. If this is the case, giving correct scores to answers which are uncertain or imprecise or adequately elicited by the examiner may lead to wrong conclusions. From a pragmatic point of view it may be useful in certain cases to adopt a more encouraging approach, to make the examinee cooperative in order to better investigate his/her potential and capabilities. Scoring, however, has to be done very carefully because the final performance will be higher than expected when using the standard procedures. We believe that the assessment phase should not frustrate the examinee, and we acknowledge the importance of developing a trusting relationship with a potential examinee. However, this must be balanced with an appropriate scoring method. Being rigorous does not imply that the examinee should not be prompted and motivated. It does mean that answers which are given only after prompting and help should not be recorded as correct, and that the fact that there was a departure from the standard procedure expected from the test administration.

From a conceptual point of view, the assignment of scores may lead (in extreme cases) to rendering a test no longer valid for interpretation. This is especially the case when the scoring is done differently from when the test was developed and normative data collected. The reason for this is straightforward: adopting a different procedure can make the test easier or more difficult, and then altering the meaning of the comparison with normative data. In addition, the evidence about the validity of a test is provided in relation to a specific administration and scoring method. Any departure from the original procedure may undermine the validity of the test for the intended purpose.

In general, scoring tests is a very delicate process. It is important to note that there are no *a priori* rules or principles about what is right or wrong in cases of ambiguities. For example, there is no *a priori* reason why self-correction should be considered in the scoring or not. The right attribution of score in these cases, is the one that was used during the development of the test. As for many other aspects treated so far, If there is no clear answer to solve an ambiguity, the examiner must take also this piece of evidence, as another detail to be taken into account in the final stage of using tests, i.e., their interpretation.

6.2 The interpretation of tests

Using a neuropsychological test involves the collection of data related to a behaviour in a structured situation, followed by scoring. After scoring (whether automatic or given by the neuropsychologist), it is important to establish what this score represents (i.e., what is being measured), and possibly to compare the score with cut-offs to establish the presence of a cognitive deficit or pathology (see Chapters 5 and 7). The most plausible meaning of the score is obviously the information about the validity of the test (discussed in section 4.2). Thus, a short-term memory test can reasonably measure short-term memory. In this section we will underline the peculiarity of this apparently trivial logical step and motivate why test results should always be *interpreted*, with the term 'interpretation' indicating here the act of explaining the meaning of the test performance. Since test results should necessarily be interpreted, the conclusions reflect the integration of different information by the neuropsychologist, who plays an active role in defining the meaning of the test results. This specific test interpretation is based on the assumptions of the Interpretative Approach (see the principles described in section 1.0).

In general, there are two situations in which the neuropsychologist has a fundamental role in interpreting tests:

1 To establish what a test actually measures in the context of a specific measurement. In this case, the key point is whether the test is valid in a specific measurement (see next paragraph);
2 To conclude whether there is a cognitive deficit. This conclusion is already part of the neuropsychological diagnosis and in particular of the *descriptive diagnosis* (see section 7.2)

6.2.1 The validity of a test for a specific measurement

The first reason why it is *necessary* to interpret a test is related to the fact that even if test scores are valid for one interpretation, this may not be the case in the context of a specific examinee.

Consider the hypothetical condition of an uncooperative examinee who is given a memory test. They may make no effort during the assessment and show no motivation, and their final score may be below cut-off. How should the test result be interpreted? Certainly, in this specific case the test cannot be considered valid for its purpose (Greher et al., 2017). There are other cases in which the measurement may not be valid for a certain purpose, such as the influence of other cognitive functions. For instance, if an examinee has a severe attentional deficit, a language test may not be appropriate to measure language abilities. Even a simple hearing loss, which is very frequent in elderly examinees, may lead to misinterpreting difficulties in auditory sensory perception as a verbal comprehension deficit linked to cognitive problems.

In a given context, the influence of spurious variables (such as sensory problems, motivation, anxiety or other cognitive functions) can alter the relationship between the construct of interest and the observed behaviour that the test is intended to measure. This issue can be considered from a different perspective. All variables other than the construct of interest potentially undermine the validity of the test for that specific measurement, i.e., a specific assessment of an examinee (see section 4.1 and Figure 4.1). The fact that for a specific measurement a test may not be considered valid explains why it is necessary to refer to '*interpretations*': test-results do not always provide the same type of information. Obviously, tests are built in such a way that they tend to provide the results for which they are valid (e.g., measuring working memory), but it is particularly important that the clinical neuropsychologist ensures that the measurement is successful.

Neuropsychological assessment can be considered as a very special measurement because cognitive functions are measured in a complex system where most of the time: 1. it is not known what may be impaired, 2. a test measuring a specific cognitive function may be influenced by other factors (other cognitive functions, anxiety, motivation, etc.). The fact that a test may not be valid in a specific measurement is particularly relevant for tests that are used with a normality cut-off. Even if a score is below the cut-off, it cannot be automatically concluded that the construct of interest is impaired (see section 5.1 for the concept of cut-off), as performance could be influenced by spurious factors. Therefore the neuropsychologist's 'interpretation' (i.e., an inference) of test results, is *always* necessary: the neuropsychologist has the crucial role of making this interpretation, and ensuring that the measurement is valid (or acknowledging that it is not).

6.2.2 Interpreting tests below the cut-off as a sign of a specific cognitive deficit

The interpretation of neuropsychological tests often aims at the identification of deficits in specific cognitive functions. To do this most neuropsychological tests rely on the comparison of observed scores with normality cut-offs (see Chapter 5).

Identifying a potential cognitive deficit is a fundamental part of the neuropsychological assessment for several reasons: a specific cognitive impairment can suggest the presence of a specific pathology, and can be the basis for a neuropsychological rehabilitation (see section 1.1). In a nutshell, in the course of the present section we will argue that an apparently clear-cut situation, as a score below the cut-off cannot be considered as conclusive evidence of a deficit in a cognitive function, as an interpretation by the neuropsychologist is always necessary.

The previous section examined how the initial active role of the neuropsychologist is to establish whether a test is valid for a specific measurement, followed by the comparison with normative data.

In Chapter 5 we have examined various cases in which the comparison with normative data may not be adequate. Firstly, an examinee may not be represented in the normative data; or a bad performance may not reflect a cognitive impairment if there are reasons to believe that the examinee may have obtained those scores before the potential damage or disorder. This may be the case if, for example, the examinee has a learning disability or low education. Similarly, a performance that is close (but above) the normality cut-off may be interpreted as a sign of deficit if the examinee has a personal and school history that leads to the expectation of an exceptionally high performance (such in the case of someone with many degrees and qualifications, or other factors suggesting high intellectual abilities). Because the role of normative data is to estimate the expected performance of an examinee (see section 5.1), in these examples the neuropsychologist may consider the normative data as not sufficiently representative.

Another possible situation is that the performance below the cut-off is due to a deficit in a cognitive function that is not the construct of interest measured by the test. For example, consider the hypothetical condition of an examinee with severe working memory problems following a head injury. If the performance is below the cut-off on several tests that do not primarily measure working memory, such as a mental calculation test, the neuropsychologist's task is to establish whether the deficit is in mental calculation or in working memory. Recognising the core deficit is crucial for rehabilitation purposes: if the examinee's deficits can be traced back to a working memory problem, training focused on this cognitive function is likely to be more effective than a specific training in calculation.

In general, compared to the situation in which only one deficit is found, the situation is more complex if there are many tests under cut-off. In these cases, there may be several distinct impairments related to the cognitive function measured by each test, or a single deficit affecting performances in all tests. This is particularly relevant if cognitive functions which are commonly involved in behavioural performance (such as attention, vigilance) are severely impaired (see Figure 4.1 and section 4.1). Such situation can be complicated, as there are no simple rules for distinguishing between different interpretations (many separate deficits vs one single core deficits affecting the whole performance). Again, the role of the neuropsychologist is to draw a conclusion from the available evidence, not only from the tests, but from all the neuropsychological assessment and the examinee's behaviour.

To summarise, if the score on a test measuring a specific cognitive function is below the cut-off, the cognitive function measured by the test may nevertheless not be impaired. Even if the impairment in the specific cognitive function is the most plausible interpretation, since the test is considered valid for this aim, there are many cases when this is not true.

6.2.3 Interpreting test results at different levels

Neuropsychological tests measure constructs at different levels: from specific cognitive functions, with a rather precise neural substrate, to broader constructs in which the neural substrate is presumably more distributed or even unknown (see section 4.1). A fundamental task of the neuropsychologist is to integrate the information coming from tests at different levels in order to interpret the results obtained. This is crucial for a diagnosis, but also for general conclusions about the examinee's cognitive status. For example, suppose that following a head injury, an examinee is assessed with a series of tests. The examinee is impaired in the FAB (Dubois et al., 2000) and in a test of phonemic fluency, but normal in several other tests that assess other aspects of executive functions. In the FAB, the examinee makes mistakes in items that are a short test of phonemic fluency. Although the FAB is a screening test that measures the general state of executive functions, for this specific case, it would not be appropriate to conclude that the examinee has 'a general deficit in executive functions'. The result on the FAB should also be interpreted in relation to the results of other tests, which assess the same construct, but at a different hierarchical level. For example, the examinee may have problems with lexical retrieval or difficulties in using search strategies presumably linked to executive functions.

Similar considerations can be made when interpreting the result on a test that does not measure a specific construct but is influenced by many heterogeneous cognitive functions. One such test is the Clock Drawing Test (Critchley, 1953) which assesses praxic abilities, memory image retrieval and planning. A performance below cut-off on the Clock Drawing Test may not indicate a deficit in all these abilities, and a correct interpretation should consider all the available information.

Some tests do not measure a specific construct or constructs, but the probability that the examinee may present with a certain pathology, such as Alzheimer's disease (see Chapter 7). These tests need to be supplemented with information from other tests for meaningful interpretation. Suppose, for instance, that an examinee's performance classifies them as likely to have Alzheimer's disease. Suppose, however, that performance on other tests is compatible with another kind of conclusion, for example related to depressive symptoms. Here, the role of the neuropsychologist is to integrate the information between the various tests to properly interpret the observed scores. In this case, the multi-level interpretation is closely linked to a different level of diagnosis (see section 8.1).

To summarise, the neuropsychologist should integrate the information from the neuropsychological tests used. The interpretation is a fundamental part of the neuropsychological diagnosis. The final product is a coherent cognitive profile characterised by preserved and impaired functions that emerge from the integration of all the information.

6.2.4 *Estimating impairments in daily life from neuropsychological tests*

During the assessment, the neuropsychologist is often asked specific questions about the examinee's daily activities (independent management of finances, fitness to drive; see also section 1.1 on the goal of neuropsychological assessment). Although there are specific tests for this purpose (e.g., The NADL-F test, Arcara et al. 2019, for assessing financial abilities), in most cases the neuropsychologist estimates impairments in daily life from tests assessing specific cognitive functions. Even if it is clear that an examinee's functioning in daily life depends on their cognitive status, conclusions of this kind should be made with extreme caution. Indeed, there are often dissociations between performance on neuropsychological tests that assess specific cognitive functions and activities that depend on those functions assessed in ecological contexts. Indeed, scores on cognitive tests predict behaviour in everyday life to a low or moderate degree (Chaytor & Schmitter-Edgecombe, 2003).

Starting from the results of neuropsychological tests, the neuropsychologist can draw conclusions about the impact that cognitive deficits may have on everyday life. In the face of very severe deficits in attention tests, it is plausible that the examinee is unfit to drive, even if the tests used do not specifically assess driving skills (attention tests assess some of the cognitive prerequisites for safe car driving).

Sometimes an examinee's difficulties in everyday life may not correspond to impaired performance in a psychometric assessment. However, the clinical setting (silence, absence of interference, a person who speaks clearly and slowly making an effort to be understood and who is interested and waiting for the examinee's answer) may promote an interaction despite a possible underlying impairment and may facilitate an examinee to obtain a performance above cut-off. However, outside the clinical setting, noise and multiple environmental stimuli may be problematic for the examinee, and explain the discrepancy between maintained performance in tests and limitations in everyday life without the consistent help of others.

From another perspective, the difficulty to perform a test is an important variable to consider in the interpretation of cognitive performance. In making conclusions about the impact of deficits in an examinee's everyday life, the neuropsychologist should be informed about the ability of the test to allow this type of predictions, through a review of the scientific literature about ecological validity or correlation with daily life activities. For example, the BADS test (The Behavioural Assessment of the Dysexecutive Syndrome) has shown evidence of ecological validity (Norris & Tate, 2000). If this information is not available, the neuropsychologist's conclusion of specific deficits in everyday life should be cautious as it may not be supported by test results.

6.3 The integration of information for interpreting tests

A key aspect in interpreting a neuropsychological test (or several tests) is the integration of all the information available to the neuropsychologist, an inferential process that leads to a diagnosis. This aspect is a crucial part of the Interpretative Approach here proposed (see section 1.0). Schematically, the critical information for the interpretation of a test can be summarised as follows:

- The first relevant information comes from the test performance itself. For example, in the case of a low score in a language test in a very distracted examinee, a qualitative analysis of performance may suggest issues with vigilance or attention, rather than with language. As argued by Goldberg and Costa (1986), the behaviour which is later coded through a score, is always much richer and more varied than any scoring system.
- Another relevant source of information are anamnestic data (see Chapter 2). These can be important not only for the diagnosis of compatibility with an aetiology (see section 8.1.2) but also for assessing the appropriateness of normative data for a given examinee. The neuropsychological interview and the preliminary neuropsychological examination, even if unstructured, can highlight many aspects that can contribute to the interpretation of the test results (for example, to identify depression), but also to highlight specific behaviours that may suggest a cognitive impairment, such as attention, memory, or language comprehension deficits. Any

impaired behaviour during the interview represents evidence to be integrated with the tests. For example, an examinee who is already very distractible in the interview may have an attention problem.

• The last source of information comes from the very important integration of the results of all tests. In a neuropsychological assessment no test result should be considered in isolation and a performance below cut-off cannot be considered as a sign of a cognitive impairment, but should always be interpreted in light of the results of the other administered test.

6.3.1 Interpreting ambiguous results

There are a number of situations in which test results could be ambiguous and particularly difficult to interpret. In the following subsections, two common ambiguous cases are examined together with some practical suggestions on how to deal with them. Importantly, the proposed solutions follow logically from the assumptions of the proposed framework and the considerations made in other chapters of the book.

6.3.2 Results close to cut-offs

A special case of ambiguity is when a result is close to cut-offs. Cut-offs are threshold values that mark the transition from one classification to another, typically from impaired to unimpaired performance.

A pointwise threshold implies that a small variation in the score (e.g., one more item with a correct or incorrect answer) can lead to a crucial difference in the outcome of the test. Therefore, in an examinee's performance one more correct item may have led to a normal performance or, conversely, one more incorrect item may have led to a pathological performance.

What should be done in such cases? A point to consider is that tests are fundamental tools, but they cannot be regarded as repositories of objective truth, as they just provide information and the fact that the performance is close to the threshold is simply another piece of information. Therefore, in the case of borderline results, or performance just below or just above the cut-off, the neuropsychologist should establish the meaning of the result. If a single result just below the cut-off is observed, perhaps within a performance on several tests in the normal range, then it is plausible that it is simply by chance (see section 4.3). On the other hand, a single borderline result in an examinee where high performance is expected given their background, may be interpreted differently and suggest further monitoring of the examinee over time to clarify the diagnosis.

In general, the key point to be considered is that there are several reasons why tests influence the accuracy of scores and the link with normative data: these may refer to features intrinsic to the test, such as reliability (see section 4.2) or they may be linked to the examinees and their personal history (see section 2.1). Such features of the measurement as well as ambiguous results should always be carefully considered by the neuropsychologist, and all the information that emerged during the neuropsychological assessment, rigorously reviewed.

6.3.3 Age or education between two different bins

In tests that use age and education tables for cut-offs it is possible that an examinee is between two different bins, with a relevant change in the cut-off between the bins (e.g., Ouvrard et al., 2019). In such cases, a difference of just one year in age can create a large change in the cut-off (from 50 to 52 years the cut-off for TMT-B changes from 40 to 45 seconds). For the interpretation of these cases we refer once again to the critical judgement of the neuropsychologist and to the meaning of the normative data, which is to estimate the performance of an examinee starting from some of their characteristics, such as age and education. A strategy that can be used in these cases is to compare the score with both cut-offs and base one's interpretation on the results of both cases. An incongruence between the performance (normal or deficient) for the two cut-offs may suggest the need of an in-depth investigation, a further monitoring over time and it certainly deserves attention by the neuropsychologist.

7 The probability of identifying a pathology in neuropsychological assessment

This chapter discusses some concepts of probabilities relevant for the neuropsychological clinical practice. Neuropsychologists often collect test scores to estimate the probability that the examinee's cognitive profile is compatible with a given disorder (e.g., a neurodegenerative disorder like Alzheimer's disease). Concepts originating from biostatistics and clinical decisions, such as sensitivity and specificity of a test, are discussed, as well as the statistical tools available to the neuropsychologist. The final part of the chapter briefly introduces Bayes' Theorem and its relevance in clinical neuropsychology. In particular, the chapter discusses how lack of knowledge of prior probabilities hampers the possibility of drawing clear-cut conclusions about probabilities from test scores. For this reason, the chapter reinforces the importance of interpreting the tests, as previously discussed in Chapter 6.

Most neuropsychological tests detect cognitive impairment by comparing the examinee's performance with normative data, i.e., data obtained in healthy people only (see Chapter 5). A score below cut-off in tests with normative data is interpreted as suggesting that a specific cognitive deficit may be present. However, the comparison with normative data and with the normality cut-off does not precisely identify the nature of a disorder, for example whether a memory deficit may be linked to Alzheimer's disease or to vascular suffering. A common request to neuropsychologists is to establish whether a specific pathology or a specific clinically condition may be present in an examinee. Due to the high incidence (and prevalence), one of the most common requests is certainly to establish whether an individual may suffer from Alzheimer's disease (i.e., show cognitive symptoms and signs compatible with Alzheimer's disease) and will therefore experience cognitive decline over time. Unlike tests that use only normative data (i.e., data on healthy people) to calculate cut-offs, some tests are able to respond directly to this type of classification demands.

DOI: 10.4324/9781003195221-7

For instance, the Mini-Mental State Examination (MMSE; Folstein, Folstein, & McHugh, 1975), which is commonly used as a screening index of cognitive functioning, was initially developed to discriminate between people with dementia, with depression and cognitive impairment, with affective disorders, and healthy people. The main feature that distinguishes tests developed to identify the presence of a condition, from those discussed in Chapter 5 is that data are collected both on healthy people and on people with a given pathological condition.

7.1 The concept of 'condition of interest'

There are several conditions that could be identified by a test. A test could be relevant to distinguish between people with probable Alzheimer's disease and people without such a disease; people who will benefit from treatment and people who will not; people with probable traumatic brain injury and people without such an injury. In each case where a (categorical) classification is requested, the method discussed in the following sections is appropriate. In more general terms, we refer to the probability of identifying an examinee with a *condition of interest* (Slick, 2006a). In the use of neuropsychological tests this typically means classifying an examinee as having a specific pathological condition.

7.1.1 A priori *division of groups and gold standards*

When developing tests in which the objective is to identify a condition of interest, it is first necessary to collect data from people belonging to one or another known group (e.g., Alzheimer's people or healthy people). By administering a specific test to these two groups it is possible to ascertain the accuracy of the test in discriminating between groups. The initial division into groups is done by using a 'gold standard', i.e., the best available procedure. In medicine, the gold standard is the most accurate procedure for identifying a condition of interest, which is often very expensive, time-consuming or invasive. In the case of neuropsychological testing, it indicates a very lengthy, or not always available procedure that is assumed to result in a very accurate detection of the condition of interest. Because of the limitations of gold-standard procedures (being time consuming or expensive), it is often useful to develop shorter, albeit less accurate, tests.

To give a concrete example, in the validation study of the Canadian version of the MoCA (Nasreddine et al., 2005) one of the goals was to calculate the sensitivity and specificity of the test in discriminating between examinees with Alzheimer's disease and healthy people. To do this, two groups of people were involved: one with and one without the condition of interest (i.e., with Alzheimer's and without Alzheimer's disease). In order to make this distinction the 'gold-standard' was the application of the DSM-IV criteria for the assessment of dementia, a rather extensive assessment. The accuracy of the MoCA in distinguishing between the two groups was then studied. Although less accurate than the gold standard, the MoCA proved to be a very fast and practical screening test.

Once data on examinees with and without the condition of interest have been collected, the accuracy of the test can be defined by reference to test sensitivity and test specificity, two well-known concepts used in medical statistics.

7.2 Sensitivity and specificity of a test

By comparing the scores of a test with a gold standard, it is possible to assess two important qualities, sensitivity and specificity:

- The sensitivity of a test is its ability to correctly identify in an examinee the presence of a condition of interest (usually a disease).
- The specificity of a test is its ability to correctly identify in an examinee the absence of a condition of interest (usually a disease).

Sensitivity and specificity are often reported as two values indicating the percentage of correctly identified 'cases', i.e., examinees with the condition of interest (e.g., sensitivity = 90% and specificity = 95%). Sensitivity and specificity are two distinct capabilities of a test, as a test could be very sensitive and very specific, very sensitive and not very specific, or very specific and not very sensitive or not very sensitive and not very specific.

If the condition of interest is a pathology, a very sensitive test correctly classifies an examinee as having a given pathology. A very specific test in turns correctly classifies an examinee as not having the pathology of interest.

In clinical neuropsychology, a 'positive test' generally indicates a low performance on a neuropsychological test, below the discrimination cut-off. Sensitivity is A/(A+C). Specificity is D/(B+D).

A test can therefore classify cases as:

- 'true positive' when the test correctly detects the presence of the condition of interest; for example, if a test classifies an examinee as Alzheimer's and that examinee actually has Alzheimer's disease, according to the gold-standard procedure;

Table 7.1 Specificity/sensitivity of a test in identifying a condition of interest (i.e., a pathology) and the outcome obtained with the classifications made by a test (see also Figure 7.1)

	Condition of interest		
	Present (e.g., examinee with a pathology)	Absent (e.g., healthy examinee)	Row total
Positive test (defective performance)	True positive (A)	False positive (B)	A+B
Negative test (adequate performance)	False negative (C)	True negative (D)	C+D
Column total	A+C	B+D	

- 'false positive' when the test incorrectly detects the condition of interest; for example, if a test classifies an examinee as Alzheimer's, but the examinee is actually healthy;
- 'false negative' when the test does not detect the condition of interest, which is actually present; for example, if a test classifies an examinee as healthy, but the examinee is actually with probable Alzheimer's disease, according to the gold-standard; or
- 'true negative' when the test does not correctly detect the condition of interest; for example, if a test classifies an examinee as healthy, but the examinee does not actually have the condition.

The ability of a neuropsychological test to correctly classify two (or more) groups of people with a pathology depends on the separability of score distribution between the two groups (e.g., very high for healthy people and very low for people with Alzheimer's disease).

Using the sensitivity and specificity of a test, it is possible to calculate a single value that allows us to distinguish optimally between the groups. Here we will call this value the *discrimination cut-off*, to avoid confusion with the *normality cut-off* (discussed throughout Chapter 5). The discrimination cut-off aims at maximising both specificity and sensitivity and refers to the probability of correctly classifying the two groups. For example, in the original study on the MoCA, the discrimination cut-off distinguishing examinees with Alzheimer's disease from healthy people is 26, with a sensitivity of 100% and a specificity of 87% (Nasreddine et al., 2005). These results indicate that a score below 26 correctly classifies 100% of Alzheimer's patients, and that scores higher than or equal to 26 correctly classify 87% of control subjects.

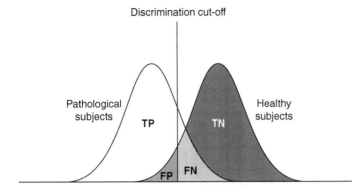

Discrimination cut-off

Figure 7.1 Possible results of a test with a discrimination cut-off. The distribution on the left indicates a hypothetical distribution of scores of people with a pathology, the distribution on the right indicates the distribution of scores of healthy people. TP = true positives, are cases of performance values below the cut-off of people who are really pathological; FP = false positives, are cases of performance values below the cut-off of people who are healthy; FN = false negatives, are cases of performance values above the cut-off of people who are pathological; VN = true negatives, are cases of performance values above the cut-off of people who are healthy.

Defining a different discrimination cut-off (e.g., lower than 26) would have increased the specificity of the test (i.e., the capacity to correctly classify healthy people), but may have decreased the sensitivity (i.e., the capacity to correctly classify people with Alzheimer's disease).

Although sensitivity and specificity are theoretically independent, for neuropsychological tests it is often the case that the more sensitive a test is, the less specific it tends to be. This is because increasing the sensitivity of a test makes it possible to increase the discrimination cut-off (referring to Figure 7.1, this would mean moving the cut-off to the right), but consequently increasing the number of false positives, that is, healthy people misclassified as having the condition of interest (i.e., the disease).

Sensitivity and specificity of a test are crucial for assessing the *criterion validity* of a test (see section 4.5.4), where 'criterion' is the presence or absence of the condition of interest. Also, a test that has acceptable sensitivity and specificity values can be considered as further support to the validity of using the test for discriminating between the conditions (see section 4.5.4). For example, the data described on the Canadian version of the MoCA support the validity of interpreting its results to distinguish between people with Alzheimer's disease and healthy people.

The normality cut-offs discussed in Chapter 5, are built only by taking into account the distribution of data from healthy people, discrimination cut-offs take into account an additional piece of information, namely the distribution of data from pathological people. Discrimination cut-offs are often determined using an analysis known as ROC (Receiver Operating Characteristic).

7.2.1 Why do only a few neuropsychological tests have sensitivity and specificity?

In the previous sections we have seen that to calculate the sensitivity and specificity of a test, two groups of examinees need to be distinguished, and this distinction is assumed to be true (by means of a procedure considered to be the gold standard).

However, in clinical neuropsychology, discrimination cut-offs are rarely available. There are two main reasons for this.

First, in clinical neuropsychology it is very difficult to identify gold standards, i.e., procedures that are unanimously considered to be the most reliable for the precise measurement of a condition of interest (e.g., a pathology). While historically the role of neuropsychology was to identify and localise brain damage (Casaletto & Heaton, 2017), the diffusion of in-vivo brain scanning (e.g., Computerised Axial Tomography, CAT, Magnetic Resonance Imaging, MRI, Positron Emission Tomography, PET) have made this role of neuropsychological testing really obsolete.

The role of neuropsychological tests has gradually shifted from detecting unobservable brain damage to identifying and describing unobservable cognitive impairments, thus without a clear gold-standard.

In the case of brain diseases, more objective techniques (like biological or imaging tests) are often available and preferred for diagnostic purposes. However, there are still cases in which a gold-standard corresponding to a pathology is a useful reference. In the previous section one such case was examined, namely the classification of people with Alzheimer's disease in which the gold standard is the application of the DSM-V criteria.[1]

The second reason is related to the fact that, in clinical neuropsychology, it is often difficult to define the 'condition of interest'. What should we do in case of a test that aims to assess whether the examinee has an impairment in a specific cognitive function, for example in short-term memory? In this case the condition of interest is the presence of a deficit in a cognitive function. In order to calculate sensitivity and specificity, we should however have an a priori gold-standard classification, which allows us to distinguish 'individuals with short-term memory impairment' from 'individuals without short-term memory impairment'. Obviously this leads us to a problem: to define accurately what is 'short-term memory impairment'. Unlike the identification of a disease, the definition of a cognitive impairment is conceptually more difficult (i.e., the gold standard should be defined by another neuropsychological test). The current approach defines an impairment as 'poor performance based on normative data', and unlikely to be observed in healthy people. For instance, an impairment in memory is defined by a poor performance (i.e., below cut-off) on the memory test obtained by healthy individuals, and not as performance from a group of examinees with a known memory impairment.

Tests that have normality cut-offs can be interpreted as tests in which only specificity is available. The normality cut-off delimiting the 5% worst scores is analogous to a test with a specificity of 95%. This aspect underlines an intrinsic limitation of tests that only refer to the normality cut-off.

Suppose we evaluate an examinee in order to establish whether their short-term memory is impaired. This objective can be reformulated in these terms: 'to try to find out whether the individual belongs to the group of people with short-term memory impairment'. Let us assume that our examinee shows a performance below the normality cut-off. What we know is only 'half the story', namely that if the individual was unimpaired, it would be unlikely to observe this performance, but it tells us nothing about what we should expect if the individual had such an impairment. Hence, it is as if we have a test where only the specificity is known. Only using data from healthy people (and therefore the normality cut-off) makes sense, because it is reasonable to assume that individuals with an impairment in a cognitive function are likely to perform more poorly than healthy individuals. The problem is that it is not known how much lower the performance should be in order to define it as impaired (and therefore to estimate a decline, see section 5.1.1).

Figure 7.2 graphically represents the information available when only normative data, i.e., data on healthy people, are available (compare it to Figure 7.1). In using this information, it is assumed that the scores of people with a cognitive impairment will have a distribution positioned more to the left (therefore with worse scores) than the distribution of healthy people. However, more precise information on this distribution is not known.

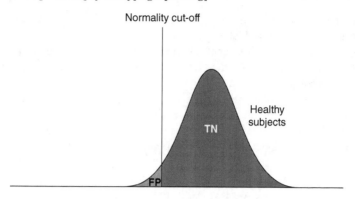

Figure 7.2 Possible results of a test with a normality cut-off. An hypothetical
distribution of scores of healthy people. FP = false positives, values below
the cut-off of healthy subjects; TN = true negatives, values above the
cut-off of healthy individuals. Compare the possible results of this
case with those of a test with discrimination cut-off, represented in
Figure 7.1.

7.3 The probability of drawing correct or incorrect conclusions in the neuropsychological assessment

The definitions of *normality cut-off* and *discrimination cut-off*,[2] implies
that the conclusions drawn from scores are never certain but are
always associated with a certain probability of error. A neuropsychologist may (or should) be interested in knowing the probability of
drawing an incorrect or correct conclusion during the neuropsychological assessment.

The above considerations suggest that the probability of making an
error is known and that in the case of the normality cut-off, the probability of making an error is 5% (in accordance to typical cut-offs for
normality, see Chapter 5).

The situation is instead much more complex because 5% indicates
the probability of making an error assuming that the examinee is
unimpaired, whereas this probability is not known if the examinee has
a cognitive impairment (see section 5.3). This problem is apparently
overcomed if a discriminative cut-off is available, as both the probability associated with belonging to a pathological group and of being
healthy are known.

However, even in the case of tests with a discrimination cut-off,
there may be issues in estimating the probability of an error. Here we
show how it is virtually impossible to estimate the probability of error
in neuropsychological assessment.

Consider these two hypothetical sentences, associated with probabilities.

1   Since the result is below the discrimination cut-off, this examinee has a 95% probability of having Alzheimer's disease.
2   95% of examinees without Alzheimer's disease score higher than this examinee.

Although they appear to be very similar, there is a significant difference between the two sentences: the first refers to the assessment of a specific examinee; the second to a general property of the test and of the examinees whose data were collected in the development of the test.

The clinical neuropsychologist is obviously interested in knowing the probability of the specific measurements of the examinee, but the available information concerns the properties of the test, and how discrimination cut-offs were constructed. A reason why it is very difficult to calculate the probability of error of a specific measurement is related to Bayes' theorem, which is described in the next section.

7.4   The importance of Bayes' theorem for the clinical neuropsychologist

Bayes' theorem is a very popular probability theorem in modern science, especially in statistics. In inferential statistics, it is the basis of the main alternative to the frequentist approach, the dominant one, which relies on p-values to determine whether a result is to be considered significant. We do not refer here to Bayesian models of statistical inference but simply to Bayes' theorem in its general formulation and its relevance to the clinical neuropsychologist (see also Crawford et al., 2009 and Huygelier et al., 2021, for practical implementations of Bayes' Theorem into clinical neuropsychology).

The main feature of the theorem is to relate different types of probabilities, in particular to clarify how certain probabilities change when new evidence is accumulated. Bayes' theorem is described by the following formula.

$$P(A \mid B) = \frac{P(A) \times (B \mid A)}{P(B)}$$

Where:

- A and B are events;
- P(A) and P(B) are the probabilities of A and B, independently of each other;

- P(B|A) (reads 'probability of B given A') is a conditional probability, specifically the probability of observing B if A is observed;
- P(A|B) (reads 'probability of A given B') is a conditional probability: the probability of observing A if B is observed.

The relevance of Bayes' theorem for the clinical neuropsychologist becomes clear if we replace the generic terms A and B with more familiar terms. Let us take a concrete example.

Suppose we assess a person with suspected Alzheimer's disease. Suppose we use a test with a discrimination cut-off to distinguish between Alzheimer's and healthy people in which the sensitivity is 95% and the specificity 85%, and that the examinee's score is below the cut-off. What is the probability that the examinee has Alzheimer given this result? The terminology introduced by Bayes' theorem allows this probability to be more clearly defined, i.e., the probability that a person has a disease. Let us denote 'A' the event 'having a disease' (e.g., Alzheimer's disease) and 'B' the event 'performance under cut-off'.[3] We now aim to find out the probability of A given B, or P(A|B)[4]. Referring to the formula of Bayes' theorem, it is clear that to estimate this probability we need to take into account also other probabilities. The situation is made clearer by making the formula more explicit for this example.

$$P(pathology \mid test\ below\ cut-off) =$$
$$\frac{P(test\ below\ cut-off \mid pathology) \times P(pathology)}{P(test\ below\ cut-off)}$$

Each probability involved in the formula can be defined:

- P(pathology|test under cut-off) is the information a clinical neuropsychologist is mainly interested in, namey the probability that the examinee has a certain pathology if the test-result is under cut-off[5];
- P(pathology) indicates the general probability of having the pathology investigated by the test, in the absence of other information. This figure could be estimated from population epidemiological data, but we will see later that this is an approximation that does not allow us to estimate the probability of correctly classifying a specific individual;
- P(test under cut-off|pathology). This piece of information corresponds to the sensitivity of the test. It is in fact the probability

of falling below the cut-off when pathology is known to be present;

- P(test under cut-off). This piece of information corresponds to the overall percentage of performance below the cut-off, irrespective of the presence or absence of pathology. In particular it can be written as P(pathology) × P(under cut-off|pathology) + P(healthy) × P(under-cut-off|healthy).

Intuitively, the great impact of Bayes' theorem in clinical neuropsychology is due to the fact that it takes into account the probability of having a disease and the accuracy of the test.

Let us again consider the test with 95% sensitivity (so P(test under cut-off|pathology) = 95%) and assume that we know the other probabilities. In particular, we assume that the disease has a prior probability of 3% (P(pathology) = 3%) and that the probability of going under the cut-off (no matter if pathological or healthy) is 8% (P(test under cut-off) = 8%).

Applying Bayes' theorem:

$$P(pathology \mid test\ below\ cut-off) = \frac{95\% \times 3\%}{8\%} \approx 35\%$$

Even if the test is very sensitive, the probability of having the disease when the test is below the cut-off is much lower than suggested by the sensitivity of the test. Furthermore, the lower the a priori probability of having the disease, the lower the probability that the person will actually have the disease, even if the test is below the cut-off.

For example, if P(disease) = 0.5%.

$$P(pathology \mid test\ below\ cut-off) = \frac{95\% \times 0.5\%}{8\%} \approx 5\%$$

These examples clearly illustrate the relevance of Bayes' theorem in clinical practice. There are however problems that limit its application. The most important one is that it is virtually impossible to calculate P(pathology) in the context of a specific assessment. P(pathology) has been defined as the generic probability of having the pathology investigated by the test. According to Bayesian terminology P(pathology) is the prior probability of having the condition, i.e., the probability in the absence of any other information.

One may consider calculating this prior probability using available epidemiological data. For example, according to past Italian epidemiological data (ISTAT, 2009), 4.1% of people over 65 years old in Italy are estimated as having Alzheimer's disease, i.e., information that can be used as P(pathology). There are however strong limitations in using this epidemiological data for this purpose because the prior probability P(pathology) changes radically depending on the context in which the test is used. Consider for example these three scenarios: 1) an assessment in a specialised centre for Alzheimer's disease 2) an assessment in the general admission to a nursing home, or 3) an assessment during a GP visit on a voluntary basis. In these three cases the prior probability (i.e., estimated even before the test-results) could be extremely different. In the first case, an examinee assessed in a specialised centre is likely to have been tested under the suspicion of having the diseases. Therefore, their prior probability of having Alzheimer's disease could be quite high. Instead, in the context of the nursing home, the probability to have cognitive impairment may be lower, as a possible reason to reach a nursing home is when independence is reduced because of cognitive decline. This probability may be intermediate to the one related to the family doctor visit, where people are assessed for general health problems.

The context thus influences the prior probability P(pathology) and consequently, referring to Bayes' theorem, it modifies the probability that is of interest to us, i.e., P(pathology|test under cut-off). Essentially, to estimate the probability of drawing correct conclusions on a specific case starting from the test-result, we should be aware of many probabilities. Some of these may be impossible to estimate and are linked to the specific context in which the test is used.

In conclusion, the clinical neuropsychologist should consider all probability data provided by a test as only indicative, rather than precise values. In order to increase the correctness of an assessment, an estimate should be made of the *prior* probabilities of an examinee having or not having a pathology or a cognitive deficit.

Notes

1. Note that not every physician and neuropsychologist would not agree to consider the DSM-V criteria as a gold standard for diagnosing Alzheimer's disease.
2. Note that in the literature there is often no clear distinction between these different types of cut-offs. The term cut-off in a test can indicate a normality cut-off, calculated only from normative data, or a discrimination cut-off, calculated to classify correctly between two or more groups.
3. Note that the probability of making a correct choice is strictly related to the probability of making a wrong choice. P(pathology|test below

cut-off) = 1 − P(pathology|test above or equal to cut-off). This is because two complementary and mutually exclusive probabilities are involved in the formula: a person can score below the cut-off or equal to or above it.

4. The terminology used here and the formulas discussed refer directly to Bayes' theorem. There is, however, an alternative (but mathematically equivalent) way of approaching this question which is based on a different terminology, specific to the diagnostic tests of Positive Predictive Value (PPV) which is equivalent to P(pathology|test below cut-off), Negative Predictive Value (NPV) which is equivalent to P(normal|test above or equal to cut-off), and base rate which is equivalent to P(pathology). In this text the more general terms associated with Bayes' theorem are used.

5. Similar considerations can be made for a test with only a normality cut-off, when the aim is to identify a cognitive deficit. In this case the reference formula would be: P(healthy | test below cut-off) = [P(test below cut-off | healthy) × P(healthy)]/[P(test below cut-off)]

8   Neuropsychological diagnosis, feedback and report

This chapter discusses the concept of the neuropsychological diagnosis, which is often the final aim of a neuropsychological assessment (see timeline, Figure 1.2). A neuropsychological assessment aims to provide a comprehensive description of an examinee's cognitive status and to guide clinical or social interventions, or rehabilitation programs. This goal significantly overturns the initial role of clinical neuropsychology which mostly aimed at inferring the presence of a neurological damage, such as a brain lesion or disease (e.g., in the case of epilepsy, see Jones-Gotman, 1991). The chapter also discusses the relationship between neuropsychological and medical diagnoses. It finally offers advice on how to provide appropriate in-person feedback to examinees and their caregivers in settings A and B and how to write a neuropsychological report.

8.1 Diagnostic reasoning and final diagnosis

The diagnostic reasoning is the process of integrating and interpreting all the information about an examinee, and specifically: 1. the anamnestic data, 2. the interview, 3. test performance, 4. any qualitative observations on the examinee behaviour, and 5. the interpretation of test results. The integration of all information in a coherent picture results in the neuropsychological diagnosis (see Figure 8.1)

In all settings, including in-person or remote interaction with a neuropsychologist (i.e., setting A and B), the diagnostic reasoning is the most delicate part of the assessment. A neuropsychologist makes a hypothesis on one or more potentially explanatory causes of the examinee's phenomenology based on the likelihood of meeting the criteria of a specific illness, also on the basis of medical information and cerebral state. This essentially requires the clinician's ability to recognise the distinctive features of a case, and to match them with a possible

DOI: 10.4324/9781003195221-8

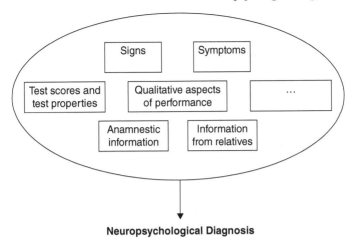

Figure 8.1 Evidence collected during the neuropsychological assessment in order to formulate a diagnosis. Altogether the information collected during the neuropsychological assessment is integrated to reach a neuropsychological diagnosis. Note, that the leftmost box mentioned test properties (e.g., validity and reliability) since they are themselves sources of information to be integrated during the diagnostic reasoning (see section 4.5.9).

pathology. If the pathology is already known (e.g., in the case of a medically diagnosed disease, such as Multiple Sclerosis, or a neurological event like a stroke or a traumatic brain injury), the neuropsychological diagnosis should draw conclusions on the compatibility of the cognitive status with the underlying diagnosis.

Providing the correct neuropsychological diagnosis depends strictly on the correctness of the information previously collected as part of the neuropsychological interview, the results of psychometric tests, the qualitative observations of behaviour and the interview with family members, and all the other information described throughout the chapters of this book. The richness of this information is fundamentally important for the diagnosis and neuropsychologists are encouraged to note any kind of relevant behaviour in an examinee during the interview and the performance in psychometric tests (Casaletto & Heaton, 2017). This should also include apparently insignificant episodes such as changes in the tone of the voice, the easiness to be distracted, the appropriateness of behaviour during testing and in the interaction with the neuropsychologist, and the perseverance in discussing the same topics in conversation. Any omission or incomplete information at any of these stages will impact on the ability to reach a precise and correct diagnostic conclusion.

Usually, diagnosis refers to a process that takes place in medicine whenever a set of symptomatic features are recognised as indicative of a specific disease. In neuropsychology, a diagnosis is a general conclusion, or an hypothesis, on causes and/or consequences of the evidence collected during the neuropsychological assessment. Providing a diagnosis implies classifying signs and symptoms in an accepted diagnostic system and identifying the neuropsychological mechanisms and factors that originated and perpetuated these signs and symptoms.

The process leading to a neuropsychological diagnosis, i.e., the diagnostic reasoning, requires the integration of all information about an examinee in a coherent pattern.

The authors of this textbook propose to distinguish the neuropsychological diagnosis in three independent levels of profiling: the Descriptive diagnosis (Level 1), the diagnosis of Compatibility with an Aetiology (Level 2) and the Functional diagnosis (Level 3). These three levels are partially independent, but the information provided is cumulative.

8.1.1 Descriptive diagnosis (Level 1)

At this first level, signs and symptoms and all the information that emerged from the clinical and psychometric assessment are summarised with a description of the cognitive status. This consists of a careful integration of all the information available in relation to the examinee and it is the starting point of the diagnostic process.

This process depends on the neuropsychologist's experience, and its active role to detect phenomena even when they are not clearly manifested, and requires the appropriate training in order to interpret them correctly. However, experience should not overshadow the neuropsychologist's unbiased perspective towards the examinee, which may prevent them from considering alternative diagnostic hypotheses at the same time. The descriptive character of this diagnosis is based on the examinee's clinical history and carefully collected information, some of which may be qualitative in nature. For instance, this may be related to the examinee's behaviour, body language and emotional reactions when examinees introduce themselves before performing the psychometric tests, or at the end of the assessment. For example, a descriptive diagnosis of executive dysfunction may be based on the observation of impaired performance in psychometric tests involving planning, organising information, logical reasoning and inhibition, as well as of distractedness and impulsivity. Importantly, drawing conclusions about a cognitive status always corresponds to a type of diagnosis (i.e., the descriptive diagnosis), as the clinician already made a number of inferences (see section 6.1 on the interpretation of tests).

8.1.2 Diagnosis of compatibility with an aetiology (Level 2)

At the second level, the neuropsychologist judges the compatibility of the observed cognitive disorders (as in Level 1) to an existing medical and aetiological diagnosis. This level of diagnosis, therefore, concerns the identification of the mechanisms and factors that underpin the neuropsychological deficit(s). For instance, neuroimaging data about the type and location of a lesion may allow a neuropsychologist to conclude that an executive dysfunction behaviour of an examinee is more likely to be the sign of fronto-temporal dementia.

Neuroimaging data can be used at this stage to describe the compatibility to some known biological and medical conditions. Note that nowadays the compatibility diagnosis tends to focus on networks, rather than specific brain areas, in contrast with the now obsolete one-to-one mapping of damage in a specific brain area with a cognitive function, which resulted in definitions such as "frontal syndrome" (Pirau & Lui 2021).

8.1.3 Functional diagnosis (Level 3)

The functional diagnosis is the third level of diagnosis which provides a prognostic prediction and a possible post-illness plan (Watt & Crowe, 2018). This depends on factors including social, economic, and environmental elements which characterise the examinee's life. The functional diagnosis is based on information collected in the descriptive and aetiological diagnosis, and can only be formulated after them.

Initially, this diagnosis refers to the level of physical and emotional independence of an examinee in order to establish whether they may be able to live autonomously in a safe way, or whether support is needed. This decision, therefore, requires considering the examinee's family and their current socio-economic environment (Bennet, 2001). In a subsequent stage, the examinee's professional situation is also evaluated to consider whether they may be able to either return to their previous occupation or may need to adjust, for instance by working in a different role, or with a different schedule. A parallel consideration has to be made for examinees who are still in education in order to decide whether and how they may be able to return to school.

8.2 Errors made by neuropsychologists in formulating a diagnosis[1]

The *Interpretative Approach* proposed in this book emphasises the importance of inferences or interpretations made from the information gathered during the whole neuropsychological assessment. Any inference or interpretation, and diagnosis itself, can be correct, incorrect or partially correct.

This is analogous to what happens in the medical field, whenever the aim is to reach a diagnosis. However, in the neuropsychological assessment there is a specific difficulty in ascertaining whether the conclusions drawn are correct or not. For example, suppose that an examinee undergoes a neuropsychological assessment to establish if a traumatic brain injury has caused some cognitive impairments. Let's suppose that the performance on some neuropsychological tests is below cut-offs and that the neuropsychologist, taking into account all the information collected in the assessment, concludes that there is indeed a cognitive impairment. How can we be sure that this is true? Keeping aside possibile considerations on malingering by the examinee (Greve et al., 2008), there is no gold-standard measure that we can use to definitively conclude that a cognitive impairment is actually present or not. This is quite different from what more commonly happens in the medical field, where feedback confirms or not a diagnosis.[2] This possibility is indeed at the core of the *ex juvantibus* (or *ex adiuvantibus*) approach to diagnosis, which in medical contexts refers to the process of making a diagnosis from the response to a treatment. For instance, if an examinee complains about abdominal pain and the physician hypotheses an inflammatory disease of the bowel, anti-inflammatory drugs can be prescribed. Should the drug be successful at alleviating the pain, this would support the correctness of the diagnosis. The important aspect, however, is that *if a drug does not work* the diagnostic hypothesis is likely wrong, and an alternative one needs to be identified.

Analogous situations are hardly applicable to the neuropsychological context, in which it is difficult to fully estimate the correctness of the conclusions drawn or the diagnosis made. A possible exception is for neurodegenerative diseases with no clear diagnosis (like Primary Progressive Aphasia, or Alzheimer's Disease), in which the neuropsychologist may reach the conclusion of a probable deterioration and then obtain a different feedback from the examinee's follow-up visits.

This issue is related to the ontological status of what is measured and assessed in clinical neuropsychology (mostly, unobservable constructs, as cognitive functions, see Chapter 4), and to the lack of objective or clear gold-standards (see also Chapter 7). The important point here is the effect of these on the neuropsychologist and on clinical neuropsychology. Without clear assessment on the own mistakes in the clinical procedure, self-correcting the practice and improving the diagnosis made are particularly difficult for a neuropsychologist (see Pezzullo 2002, for an interesting paper on how neuropsychologists can be cheated).

Difficulties in ascertain the correctness (or not) of a diagnosis and the overall quality of the interpretations made during the neuropsychological assessment hampers the methodological progresses in clinical neuropsychology, both with respect to constructs (see section 4.1), and the selection of the best tests to be employed (see section 4.6).

8.3 Feedback to the examinee

Feedback can be provided at two main points in time, during and at the end of an assessment. Both types of feedback are essential aspects of the relationship between the examinee and the neuropsychologist. However, in the first case, the feedback aims to reassure and motivate an examinee to carry out the neuropsychological examination, whereas feedback at the end serves the purpose to inform the examinee of the general outcome of the examination.

8.3.1 Feedback during the assessment

During the psychometric assessment, examinees often expect a partial account of their performance. A good practice is to be empathic and supportive to maintain a good relationship with the examinee, and avoid being distant and aseptic, and also patronising. For example, if a rather anxious examinee asks worriedly about their performance during an assessment in settings A, the neuropsychologist could answer: "A number of things were done well, and a few a little less well, but do not worry, try to keep it up". On very few occasions, for instance, in very compromised examinees, a neuropsychologist may want to be supportive even if they failed a test completely. In setting C, feedback during the assessment is not always provided and may consist of general and shorter encouragement (e.g., "Keep it up!", "Well done so far!").

The feedback during the assessment is particularly useful for examinees who are assessed for the first time, and therefore may be concerned about the outcome of the examination, and may even be reluctant to continue with it if they feel it is too uncomfortable. This is why the assessment should not be a rigid sequence of questions with long pauses for answers, with embarrassing silences between each one, but a fluid flow of a dialogue within which the examiner is able to record the answers and eventually score them.

8.3.2 Feedback at the end of the assessment (on the preliminary analysis of the results)

At the end of the assessment, the neuropsychologist is ready to provide feedback, which is typically expected by the examinee (see timeline, Figure 1.2). The examinee should be acknowledged for the time and effort made, as well as for coping with the demands of the assessment.

The type of feedback provided depends on the type of examinee and can range from a simple reassurance and smile, letting the examinee go back to their family, to an in-depth discussion about the assessment directly with the examinee. The first situation occurs when the examinee is mostly unaware of their cognitive state (anosognosia) and usually cognitively very impaired, typically in settings A and B. In these anosognosic examinees, feedback may persuade them to consider entering possible rehabilitation programs or to accept support.

The second situation typically occurs with examinees with mild deficits who are aware and concerned about their future, and who may tend to amplify their deficits and suffer from depression as a consequence of this. The neuropsychologist's feedback, therefore, may help to rescale the problem by emphasising the positive factors in the examinee's performance, which may also persuade them to accept support to cope with their problems.

In other words, the neuropsychologist should never deny an examinee's feeling, but accept it at least partially and then gradually modify the extent of the examinee's failed perception: "I understand what you say, and I understand your feeling of inadequacy. Although it was not a brilliant performance, I assure you that it did not go badly at all. You could do even better than that next time, you're right".

Another point to highlight is that the neuropsychologist should never lie about the outcome of the examination, either to avoid increasing the state of anxiety or depression or on the contrary to decrease the state of awareness. In the case of an examinee with an advanced deterioration, the feedback must always be reassuring, to avoid eliciting anxious states that would increase confusion and psychomotor agitation, without leading to any benefits.

In setting C, the feedback is usually provided at the completion of a test by the software used to run the tasks. The feedback can be relatively general (e.g., "Well done!"), or can be more specific, for instance by providing the number of correct answers. No direct communication with the neuropsychologist occurs in this setting.

Overall, the feedback therefore provides encouragement and information to the examinee, and for settings A, and B is also the ending point of the diagnostic reasoning, before completing the formal report.

8.3.3 Examples of feedback to the examinee

All the examples below are suitable for settings A, and B (with in-person or remote interaction for the neuropsychologist). The paraverbal and non-verbal features (prosody, body language, voice) reported in brackets at the beginning of each exchange are a pure exemplification and should be adapted depending on the setting and the context.

8.3.3.1 Example 1. Feedback providing reassurance to an older examinee with an advanced degenerative disease

P: [*Looking confused, fidgeting with his fingers, and seating rigidly on the edge of the chair*] So, how did I go?

NPS: [*Looking reassuring, keeping eye contact and moving closer to the examinee – based on aetiological diagnosis*] Well, what I can tell you at the moment, is that there are some difficulties that we need to monitor. However, things are still well under control, and I would suggest accepting the support of your family, so your life can continue as usual for as long as possible. What do you think?

P: [*Looking more relaxed, seating more comfortably, and leaning on the back of the chair*] So, this is not too serious, right? and I can continue to live with my family?

NPS: [*With a firm voice and nodding*] Of course you can! But as I mentioned there are some issues so it would help if you accept help and support to make sure you can carry out your usual activities as long as possible.

8.3.3.2 Example 2. Feedback providing practical information about returning to work to a younger examinee living with consequences of a brain injury

P: [*Sounding positive and looking confident*] So, how did it go, was it ok, right?

NPS: [*With a firm and confident voice, looking at the results to support their statements, sitting straight with arms on the desk – based on descriptive diagnosis*] Well, yes, as you saw, there were many positive results because you did well in a number of tests, especially the computerised ones. However, the results that we obtained in some specific tests show that there are still difficulties, for instance in responding to items based on their appearance or their sound, or in paying attention. Does it make sense?

P: [*Looking gratified and with a cheerful voice*] Yes, I really enjoyed working on the computer. So, it wasn't so bad after all, wasn't it?

NPS: [*Sitting still, minimising arms' and hands' movements, and using a firm voice to clarify the examinee's difficulties, including their inability to recognise them – based on functional diagnosis*] Yes, as I said it was not too bad, but nevertheless there were some difficulties which are likely to make it hard to go back to work in the near future or to drive a car. It would help to continue with the rehabilitation program you started. What do you think? Shall we meet in three months time to review the situation and you will tell me if the rehab has helped?

P: [*Looking reassured when told about a deadline to review the situation, still sitting comfortably and sounding optimistic*] Sure, three months sounds like a good time!

NPS: [*Looking unsure that the examinee fully understood the importance and impact of their problems and yet sounding positive*] Excellent! We can certainly tailor the rehabilitative intervention to focus on the activities that are likely to be most relevant for your own work and life. How does it sound?

P: [*Answering briefly and with little involvement*] That seems like a good plan!

8.4 Feedback to the family

If an examinee is accompanied by a family member or a carer, meeting them is very important and at the same time an extremely delicate moment of the whole assessment. Since this meeting aims – among others – to provide feedback about the examinee's situation, it should be conducted after the assessment, and preferably without the examinee, unless this raises issues such excessive suspicion, or it hampers the neuropsychologist-patient or family-patient relationship.

The feedback of a preliminary diagnosis can trigger a variety of reactions by an examinee's family members. For example, in response to the news of an examinee's illness, family members may initially deny or play down the presence of disturbances or abnormalities in daily life, and only later accept the diagnosis (Gruters et al., 2021).

This may be exacerbated by possible changes in the family status or in terms of roles in the family dynamics. For instance, pathologies that affect the emotional or financial independence of an examinee imply that other family members need to cover these roles. For example, financial responsibilities may have to be sustained by a spouse who otherwise would expect this role to be taken up by the partner, or parental duties may be too challenging for an adult with an illness, leaving their children confused and with less parental guidance.

For these reasons, the feedback of a preliminary diagnosis requires a high level of clinical competence by a neuropsychologist in order to provide accurate information, as well as support to the emotions of the examinee and the family members (Gruters et al., 2021). The neuropsychologist also needs to provide concrete suggestions to manage the post-illness situation in the acute and chronic stages of the illness.

The feedback to the family aims to:

1 Provide a preliminary diagnosis. This is based on an initial inspection of the outcome of the assessment, before a full analysis is carried out. The neuropsychologist provides the family with a description of the main characteristics of the disorder, the possible cognitive and behavioural difficulties of the examinee rather than communicating a diagnostic label (aetiological diagnosis).

   This feedback of a preliminary diagnosis is an important part of the whole assessment and can trigger a variety of reactions by an examinee's family members. For example, in response to the news of an examinee's illness, family members may initially deny or play down the presence of abnormalities in daily life, and only later accept the diagnosis. This may be exacerbated by possible changes in the family status or in terms of roles in the family dynamics.

   If a diagnosis has already been made, the initial feedback aims to help the family to face the expectations, forecasts and hypotheses related to the illness (Functional diagnosis). This is particularly important when the relatives themselves request a neuropsychological assessment for the examinee, and it is therefore important to provide the family with the correct interpretation of some unusual behaviours. For example, by explaining that the verbal and sometimes physical aggression is not due to hostility towards them, but is a symptom linked to the organic condition following the neurological disease or brain injury (e.g., Stimmel et al., 2019).

2 Obtain further information about the examinee's behaviour at home or in other contexts, which is essential for a complete and correct neuropsychological assessment.

During the meeting, the neuropsychologist enquiries about an examinee's current and past (prior to the lesion or pathology) personality and habits or behavioural disorders. These are relevant for the neuropsychological assessment, and they may also have a repercussion within the family. Sometimes, changes may be subtle and a family may not be fully aware of them, and in other cases a family may be embarrassed or ashamed to report inadequate and emotionally disturbing behaviours. A neuropsychologist therefore needs to be tactful and at the same time ask straight questions, such as: "Is (the examinee) sometimes apathetic?" or "Is s/he irritable?" or "Is s/he sometimes aggressive?". They should never be inquisitorial, but rather try understanding the examinee's issues.

3 Verify the correctness of the information provided by the examinee. This is important especially in situations where examinees are not aware of the clinical conditions, and also when examinees try to simulate a situation different from their own, often showing a more positive light, for instance to cover some difficulties they may have.

4 Provide support. The feedback also aims to acknowledge the problematic nature of the examinee's disorder and the difficulties in managing it. The neuropsychologist should also be able to provide family members with simple strategies for managing day-to-day challenges. Offering support to family members helps them to better understand an examinee's illness and in turn it may also help others outside the household to become aware of the situation.

8.4.1 Examples of feedback to the family

8.4.1.1 Example 1. Feedback providing information (to the family of an examinee with clear signs of a degenerative disease)

In attendance: Wife and daughter (family, F) of the examinee, meeting the neuropsychologist (NSP) for the first time.

F: [*With anxious expression, looking nervous, fidgeting with the handbag, and sitting rigidly on the edge of the chair*] So, what was he like, how did he go?

NPS: [*With a clear and calm voice, looking directly at the examinee, keeping arms unfolded and sitting straight. Delivering descriptive diagnosis*] Well, your doctor will provide a proper diagnosis, however, what the assessment showed is that there are clear difficulties in memory, in finding words and orientation in time and space. Did you also notice these difficulties?

F: [*Feeling involved in the conversation, and actively responding. Less nervous*] Yes, at the beginning we thought this was just ageing, but we then noticed that difficulties increased progressively, even in relatively simple activities. For instance, until a few months ago, my husband was in charge of paying the bills at the post office. Then he started to be reluctant and came up with unreasonable excuses, and finally he refused altogether. This is something he used to enjoy as it also meant meeting and chatting with people he knows well, and also going for a walk, which he has always enjoyed. Now he has completely changed.

NPS: [*Looking attentive at the family's words, and mirroring their words to indicate empathy and good understanding. Delivering the aetiological diagnosis*] Yes, I understand. It sounds that your husband was a very active and extroverted man.

F: [*With an animated voice*] Yes, he was! And he has always been so supportive too.

NPS: [*With an emphatic tone and looking serious*] Of course. And it is very hard to understand and accept these changes. Unfortunately, all these difficulties do not just reflect ageing but they are likely to depend on a brain pathology, which typically affects some cognitive abilities and is progressive, I'm afraid.

F: [*Looking confused and again a bit anxious*] Ah, progressive.... This means....

NPS: [*Sounding professional, and avoiding a patronising tone*] Well, this means that it is likely that these difficulties will be more frequent and more severe.

F: [*Sounding anxious again, and looking tearful*] And do we know how fast this may be?

NPS: [*Maintaining a professional tone while sounding emphatic*] At the moment we do not know. He may decline rapidly or he may be stable for some time, it is hard to predict but we will monitor him regularly.

F: [*With a sparkle in their voice and looking positive*] Ok, I understand.... Are there any treatments that may help to stop or at least slow down the decline?

NPS: [*With a clear voice and maintaining good eye contact, avoiding unnecessary gesturing*] Your GP will discuss the treatments with you. However, current treatments control the more severe symptoms but they cannot stop the progression of the disorder. In other words, they can ameliorate the symptoms but they cannot make them disappear.

F: [*Feeling reassured and well-informed, seating more comfortably and leaning on the back of the chair*] Ok, we understand. And how should we prepare practically?

NPS: [*With a clear voice to deliver the functional diagnosis*] Well, first of all it is important to understand that moving forward your husband and father would need constant support and supervision on a daily basis. It is also very important to understand that he is not responsible for these difficulties, and therefore avoid making him feel guilty for them.

F: [*With a firm voice and showing some reassurance*] Sure, we understand. How do we leave things now?

NPS: [*Assertive and practical, speaking slowly to avoid overwhelming the family with information*] So, I will arrange a visit with your general practitioner (GP) who will prescribe the medication. I can also put you in touch with support groups guided by a psychologist, where caregivers in similar situations share their experiences and provide information and support. How does it sound?

F: [*Sounding more positive*] It seems like a good idea.

NPS: [*With clear voice, showing involvement*] Another thing that you may want to consider are some treatments based on cognitive stimulation such that all the current cognitive skills are reinforced so that they can be maintained for as long as possible. Your GP will discuss these with you.

F: [*Looking thoughtful but grateful for being well informed*] Many thanks for your help.

NPS: [*Smiling, with a warm and emphatic voice, standing up ready to shake their hand and to accompany them to the door*] You are welcome. See you soon.

8.5 Neuropsychological report

8.5.1 Content of the report

After a neuropsychological assessment, a clinical report should be written. This report documents what has been done during the neuropsychological examination, it states the diagnostic conclusions and possible alternative interpretations, and it comments on any limitations of the results. If possible, the report should be drawn up immediately after the examination because this is the optimal time to describe in an exhaustive form the conclusions on a neuropsychological case by integrating the quantitative and qualitative data actively collected during the assessment.

A neuropsychological report should include:

1　All the information available about the examinee from external sources (e.g., medical or neuropsychological examinations, information from the family)
2　All the information gathered directly from the examinee in the interview, the qualitative observations, and the results of the psychometric tests;
3　The neuropsychological diagnosis, which includes the description of the examinee's cognitive state and its compatibility with a possible underlying pathology. This also includes a table with the scores obtained, the corresponding normative data and the reference of the material used.

In the case of impairments so severe to prevent the administration of tests, a table containing mostly null values should be replaced by a qualitative description of the examinee's behaviour. This may report the examinee's interaction with the neuropsychologist and also with the environment.

The report should also clearly address the specific referral request. For example, if the neuropsychological examination is preliminary to a rehabilitation treatment, a suggestion should be made of a possible intervention to be carried out, including a description of the objectives to pursue and predictive outcomes. Likewise, when the purpose of the examination is to assess fitness to drive, the report should include a clear statement as to whether the cognitive prerequisites to drive a car safely are met.

8.5.2 Style of the report

A neuropsychological report has no standard format, but must be complete and concise. It should state the clear purpose of the examination and indicate the information available to the neuropsychologist while carrying out the examination, summarise the results of the assessment, and contain a conclusion concerning the cognitive state of the examinee (i.e., the diagnosis). The delivery of the report may be preceded by a verbal communication as part of the feedback (feedback at the end of the assessment, based on a preliminary analysis of the results; see timeline, Figure 1.2).

According to the Interpretative Approach, the report should be compiled by the person who has directly observed and assessed the examinee (see the principles described in Chapter 1), although in some cases and contexts other professionals can administer the tests, but not write the report (Harvey, 2012). It should be easily readable and understandable, and contain unequivocal conclusions that are not subject to misunderstandings; it should be designed with the examinee and their family in mind, their needs and their level of understanding.

A key feature of the report is that it needs to succinctly summarise solely the results which are relevant for the diagnosis, avoiding unnecessary details. It should also avoid reporting a simple list of cognitive deficits directly reflecting the tests' scores in absence of a coherent diagnostic profile.

Non-standardised nosographic constructs or categories should not appear in the report, unless there are clear bibliographic citations, and the language should be neither technical nor slang, but simple and clear with essential syntax. It is important to specify the different sources from which the information, data and procedures used to collect the data come from, for example, interviews with the examinee, with their family, psychometric tests, questionnaires, etc. It is essential to always include the bibliographic citations from which the tests or questionnaires derived, and the normative data used for the conclusion.

It is important to underline that the report should not be a mere description of the behaviour, but it should be intertwined with the interpretation of the results. For example the neuropsychologist could write in the section on the interview: "the examinee keeps using swear words throughout the examination, suggesting lack of inhibition". Although these interpretations are optional in most of the sections, they should be mandatory in the section describing the neuropsychological diagnosis.

8.5.3 Tips on how to write a report

The preparation of the report is usually facilitated by using a standard grid containing the essential questions a neuropsychologist needs to obtain from an examinee, with flexibility depending on the type of examinee and examination.

A critical point of this structure is the way in which the cognitive information is categorised because the results of a test may reflect more than one cognitive ability at a time. For instance, a Picture Naming Test aims to measure an examinee's ability to retrieve the name of the depicted objects, and could be reported under the cognitive function 'language'. However, before naming the objects, this task also assumes their correct recognition, and impairments in doing so should be reported under the cognitive function 'Visual recognition'. It is, therefore, better to avoid making a rigid subdivision of the cognitive functions on the basis of the tests. Grouping into categories of cognitive functions can be of help for the readability of the report, but it is important to keep in mind that every test is often multidimensional and related to several cognitive functions (Lezak, 2000; Bell & Roper,1998).

A table, which should be part of the report template available, should include a list of all the possible psychometric tests available to perform. This list is then adapted by the neuropsychologist depending on the specific examination, and reporting only the tests currently used.

Table 8.1 illustrates how the diagnostic process integrates all information about an exemplary case and how this is included in the report.

8.5.4 *Ethical considerations*

Clinicians in their role of neuropsychologist should comply with the Code of Ethics of their country. This usually contains legal indications concerning the protection of the person being assessed, the recognition of their rights and respect for privacy. They establish the person's right to be informed about the assessment and its potential outcome, and to negotiate their intervention and express consent. Sometimes it is only the examinee who is involved, other times their family or the legal tutor are involved, especially when the examinee's cognitive capacities are limited or the examinee is under age.

Concerning the report, it must be accurate in its form and terms because it strongly commits the professional responsibility of the neuropsychologist who undersigns it, both from a legal and deontological point of view (Hanson & Kerkhoff, 2018).

It is the neuropsychologist's responsibility to ascertain the validity and reliability of the test used and the robustness of the data collected.

The neuropsychologist is strictly bound to professional secrecy. Therefore, they shall not disclose news, facts or information acquired as a result of their professional relationship. The neuropsychologist shall not misuse the available diagnostic and assessment tools, for example by drawing conclusions on a cognitive ability based on failure in tests not measuring that ability, or due to misunderstanding of task instructions rather than actual underperforming. When reports are commissioned by third parties, the neuropsychologist shall inform the examinees about the nature of their professional intervention and shall not inappropriately use the information learned, except within the limits of the mandate received.

On the other hand, the neuropsychologist needs to protect their professional and clinical role by ensuring that the content of the report is not used inappropriately, or in the inappropriate context. To this aim, a statement may be added to the report itself, for instance saying that "This report has been completed for clinical purposes only,

Table 8.1 How the diagnostic process integrates all information about an exemplary case (GC) and how this is included in the report.

Sections of the Report	Information to be included	Example	Key information for diagnostic reasoning
A. Before meeting the examinee: Information from external sources			
Examinee's personal data	• Name • Date of birth • *Sex* • Handedness • Address • *Civil status* • Living situation (alone, with family /carer) • GP	Mrs GC 15/08/1939 - 76 years old, F 2, New Road, London N8 7YT Married, three sons. Living with husband; lived in different cities to follow her husband, a bank manager Kindland Medical Practice	• Living with husband → There is support
Examination context	• Date and time of the examination • Place of the examination • Who performs the examination • Reason for referral, who referred the examinee • How an examinee got to/ dealt with the appointment (accompanied or alone)	22/01/2016, 9:00 am General hospital Dr. Mondini Geriatrician requested cognitive assessment for suspected decline. Mrs GC arrives accompanied by her husband but remains alone for the visit.	• Suspected decline
Available Documentation	Clinical examinations/ medical tests (blood/hormonal tests, vitamin intake)	Normal cholesterol values; no diabetes.	Cholesterol within the norm → Regular physiological functioning

(Continued)

Table 8.1 How the diagnostic process integrates all information about an exemplary case (GC) and how this is included in the report. *(Continued)*

Sections of the Report	Information to be included	Example	Key information for diagnostic reasoning
	Neuro-imaging examinations	Brain CT scan for possible minimal ischemic changes and mild atrophy.	Mild atrophy → May be a normal age-related condition
	Neurological or psychiatric examination	Geriatrician report: Dr Green, 13/01/16, "The examinee complains mainly of tiredness, lack of interest for previously enjoyable activities; frequent anomias confirmed by her husband".	• Lack of interest → Possible depression? • Frequent anomias → Cognitive impairment?
	Previous neuropsychological assessments	None.	No baseline data available
	Medical history (past hospitalizations, neurological history)	1999: Heart-related surgery (mitral and tricuspid plastic surgery and closure of the foramen ovale). 2011: Pacemaker. Previous unilateral cataract operation. Since 2015: hypothyroidism under treatment. 2015: episode of mental confusion, probably associated with heat stroke.	• Cardiac problems • Suspected transient ischemic attack → May indicate cardiovascular disorders which may affect cerebral functioning, and hence lead to cognitive impairment.
	Pharmacological treatment	Euthyrox for treatment of hypothyroidism. Cardio aspirin.	• Cardio aspirin → Cardiovascular disorders?

(Continued)

Table 8.1 How the diagnostic process integrates all information about an exemplary case (GC) and how this is included in the report. *(Continued)*

Sections of the Report	Information to be included	Example	Key information for diagnostic reasoning
B. Meeting the examinee **(Anamnesis & neuropsychological semiotics)**			
Neuropsychological interview	Psychological history (traumatic events, stress, depression, anxiety)	None reported	
Neuropsychological and Psychometric Examination	Cognitive history (education, working activity, leisure time activity)	• Graduated from classics high school, and attended Art school for a few years. • Housewife. • Loves the mountains and walking; avid reader; she listens to music and often goes to the theatre. • Average cognitive reserve level, 104 (CRIq, Nucci et al, 2012)	• Cognitive reserve is of average level → Predict average cognitive performance considering age and education
Interview with the family/caregiver	• Life Habits (sleeping and eating habits) • Mood and behaviour	• Normal appetite; good diet; takes regular sleeping tablets • Detectable signs of non-pathological anxiety during the assessment	

(Continued)

Table 8.1 How the diagnostic process integrates all information about an exemplary case (GC) and how this is included in the report. *(Continued)*

Sections of the Report	Information to be included	Example	Key information for diagnostic reasoning
Psychometric assessment	Performance of the examinee and scoring in the administered tests, and appropriate comparison to the normative data.	Performance often within the normal range, but laborious, for example, target objects incorrectly named a number of times before reaching the correct outcome; frequent fluctuations, for example, some target stimuli remembered straight away whereas others taking much longer. TMT-B performed correctly but took longer than expected based on normative data. Maintained orientation in space and time	• Performance within the lower limit of the normal range → May indicate the initial stage of cognitive decline • Fluctuations in performance may also reflect mood changes and anxiety → Need monitoring and possible follow-up assessment
Interview with the carer (when possible)	Information regarding day-to-day living and other noticeable changes	Changes in housekeeping; less independence in going out or making decisions; occasional forgetfulness and tearfulness (not previously observed), increased sadness.	Increase in frailty and possible mood change.

(Continued)

Table 8.1 How the diagnostic process integrates all information about an exemplary case (GC) and how this is included in the report. *(Continued)*

Sections of the Report	Information to be included	Example	Key information for diagnostic reasoning
C. After meeting the examinee (diagnosis)			
Neuropsychological Diagnosis	Conclusions containing the neuropsychological diagnosis with particular attention to the referral request.	The neuropsychological assessment revealed the presence of fluctuating cognitive difficulties mainly affecting the executive and control functions, which also emerged in language. The psychometric scores (see Table below) are within average, but a qualitative analysis of performance suggests a fluctuating cognitive impairment, compatible with a cognitive disorder, addressing the request of the referral. It would be useful to repeat the neuropsychological assessment in 6 months.	• Collect all previous information in a coherent manner; • Summarise the main findings for the examinee/ carers • Suggest a possible diagnosis based on neuropsychological examination and medical information • Provide suggestions on future plans
Table with raw and scaled scores	Psychometric scores Normative data (matched for age, education, gender, cognitive reserve or other) Comparison of the examinee's scores with norms Bibliographical references of the tests and normative data.	See examples of Tables in Chapter 9.	See diagnostic conclusions above

and at the request of the person concerned, to whom it is addressed". Exceptions to this are cases of advanced cognitive impairments, such as dementia, whereby the conclusions of the report cannot be exploited by the examineé. A similar cautious approach should be used in cases of symptom simulation in which personally handing over a report to an examinee may indirectly and unfairly facilitate obtaining disability or accompaniment allowance.

The law and regulations may change depending on the context of the neuropsychological assessment and may be specific to the country or to the national health system, or the professional associations' regulations.

8.6 Conclusions

In this present book we have proposed the Interpretative Approach as a framework for the clinical neuropsychological assessment in which methodological aspects and practical considerations are strictly interconnected. With this aim, we presented the sequence of steps in a typical neuropsychological assessment, from the collection of anamnestic data to the interview, the administration of tests, and the outline of the report with the diagnosis.

The Interpretative Approach emphasises the key role of the neuropsychologist (rather than the instruments used) stressing the importance of the neuropsychologist's interpretation throughout the whole assessment. The reader can embrace the overall approach or focus on specific aspects, which can be easily incorporated and adapted into clinical practice. The book overall aims to increase the neuropsychologist's awareness of clinical practices, and to develop a clearer understanding of methodological concepts at the basis of the neuropsychological assessment. This awareness can in turn refine the neuropsychologists' expertise and the quality and accuracy of the assessment.

Notes

1. This paragraph is largely inspired by a lesson given by Corrado Lo Priore, in a post-graduate Master's course on clinical neuropsychology held in Padua (Italy) in 2006.
2. The authors acknowledge that this is a simplification. As always in medicine, there are many cases in which it could be very difficult to reach a clear-cut conclusion about the correctness (or not) of the diagnosis. This, however, typically occurs with diseases characterised mostly by subjective symptoms (e.g., migraine, fibromyalgia, etc.).

9 Examples of clinical cases and reports

This chapter provides a series of detailed and practical examples of neuropsychological cases including the examinees' personal history (i.e., medical, psychological and cognitive), the assessment and the final report. As such, this chapter exemplifies the concepts previously introduced with real cases taken from the clinical experience of the authors.

The examples given are very heterogeneous, in order to make clear the wide applicability of the neuropsychological investigation. The examples provided illustrate the use of the different settings (A, B, and C).

Here we report two cases of assessment: the first of a well known and documented clinical condition, the second with no clinical documentation available (e.g., results of previous clinical or neuropsychological examinations). Only the perception of changed cognitive conditions was reported by the caregiver. For those cases, we provide a short introduction to the report. In all cases, we fully explain the *diagnostic reasoning,* namely the assessment and diagnostic process that the neuropsychologist carried out during and after the examination.

9.1 A case of head trauma: in-person setting with paper-and-pencil tests (Setting A)

This case aims to evaluate the cognitive consequences of a severe head trauma through the exclusive use of a standard paper-and-pencil test battery. This was based on setting A, where there is a direct interaction of the examinee with the neuropsychologist who monitors the testing as well as the examinee's behaviour from a face-to-face perspective. In this case, setting A was preferred to others due to the severity of the examinee's condition, and his distractibility, in particular, which precluded the use of a remote (setting B) or remote self-assessment (setting C, see section 1.3).

DOI: 10.4324/9781003195221-9

9.1.1 Information used by the neuropsychologist for the diagnosis

9.1.1.1 Case description

Mr Peter White is a right-handed 41-year-old man who had a head trauma following a car accident in July 2016; before then, he lived with his partner; he has a child who lived with his ex-wife. He has 13 years of education, following which he worked as a freelance business consultant in the family company.

Mr White came to the neuropsychology clinic (setting A) as an in-patient on the recommendation of his neurologist, once the acute phase following the accident (with a brain hematoma, and uncontrolled behaviour) had passed. This initial neuropsychological assessment aimed to describe the neuropsychological profile in order to provide information useful to plan a tailored rehabilitation program. The latest CT scan (01/07/16) revealed hypodense areas in the left parietal, temporal and bilateral frontal sites.

9.1.1.2 Information from the neuropsychological anamnesis

Mr White arrived accompanied by his mother for the neuropsychological examination. He showed residual motor impairment in his right arm (fractured). During the neuropsychological interview, he showed clear impulsivity in answering questions which reflected possible attentional deficits, very fast but inaccurate speech, often not well understandable. He claimed to be ready to return to work, showing some level of unawareness about his physical and cognitive condition.

Mr White mentioned that he had always led an active lifestyle, with a strong passion for sports including sensation-seeking activities such as gliding or speleology. The CRIq (Cognitive Reserve Index questionnaire, Nucci et al., 2012), a questionnaire that provides an index of cognitive reserve, was administered. The Cognitive Reserve level was 114 which is within the upper average of the population, scoring between 85-114. Mr White's CRIq reflected his leisure's activities rather than his education or working activities.

The psychometric assessment started using a standard paper-and-pencil battery, useful to get a general idea of the cognitive and behavioural difficulties (setting A). Because of motor impairment and attentional deficits only traditional rather than digital tests were used. The outcome of the assessment was consistent with Mr White's behaviour during the interview.

9.1.1.3 Information from the psychometric assessment

The neuropsychologist's accurate observation of the examinee during the tests showed impulsivity, lack of inhibition, perseverative behaviour, rigid reasoning, impaired abstract reasoning and attentional deficits. Furthermore, he showed memory deficits due to retrieval difficulties. Language impairment was related to pragmatics.

He had a certain degree of anosognosia, being unaware of his deficits.

The lesion site documented is mainly related to the frontal areas.

The description of his behaviour made from the caregiver/mother reported behavioural disinhibition.

Information from the caregiver

Mr White's mother was interviewed in order to provide her account of the case. She reported Peter's very uncontrolled behaviour with impulsive answers and unawareness of his capacities. For instance, she reported his intention to return home from the hospital and directly back to work.

9.1.2 Chronological step-by-step diagnostic procedure

The assessment aimed to describe the examinee's cognitive difficulties and their origin, and to identify areas of maintained functioning in order to formulate a tailored cognitive rehabilitation treatment.

Step-by-step reasoning (see Table 9.1)

Step 1: Before meeting the examinee

Existing anamnestic data (premorbid normal cognitive functioning, reported traumatic brain injury primarily involving frontal areas, demographic information such as age),

Step 2: Meeting the examinee
- Neuropsychologist's observations during the initial interview with the examinee (impulsivity, uncontrolled speech, difficulties in following the conversation);
- Psychometric assessment (difficulties in tests assessing inhibitory processing, verbal and non-verbal reasoning, verbal fluency);
- Carer's report (suggesting unawareness of his own condition, and lack of organisation of his daily living)

Step 3: Neuropsychological diagnosis

Collectively, the information from the anamnesis, the psychometric examination and the caregiver's report, was compatible with an aetiological diagnosis of dysexecutive syndrome which is observed quite frequently after head trauma.

9.1.3 Report of the neuropsychological assessment

Personal data

Mr Peter White, DoB: 21/04/1975 (41 years old), Male, right-handed (currently he cannot move the right arm correctly)
   Address: ...
   Divorced, living alone, his partner left him alone
   GP: Dr X

Examination context

Date and time: 02/05/2016, 9:00 AM.
   Place:
   Who performs the examination: Dr X, neuropsychologist
   Reason and source of referral: request from intensive care neurologist to treat the behavioural and cognitive dysfunctional profile following the acute phase of his head trauma.
   How an examinee got to the appointment: Mr White was an inpatient who arrived at the examination accompanied by his mother but he was on his own during the neuropsychological examination. He was cooperative throughout.

Available documentation

Medical record including neuroimaging reports (CT scan reporting hypodense areas in the left parietal and temporal regions, as well as bilateral frontal). In the acute phase, cognitive reports indicate the examinee's state of confusion and lack of behavioural inhibition.

Neuropsychological anamnesis

Medical history: no specific events to report.
   Pharmacological treatment: current anti-epileptic medication.
   Psychological history: no specific events to report. The examinee lives on his own and has limited family support, the examinee's mother being the main carer.
   Cognitive history: education up to A-level (13 years). The CRIq (Cognitive Reserve Index questionnaire, Nucci et al., 2012) level was 114 which is within average range (corresponding to a score between

85-114). Mr White's CRIq reflected his leisure's activities rather than his education or working activities. He reported having an active life-style, a passion for sports including sensation-seeking activities such as gliding, or speleology.

Life habits: good appetite and regular sleeping pattern.

Mood and behaviour: adequate and stable during the assessment. There was, however, certain irritability during the conversation with his mother. At a behavioural level, qualitative observations during the administration of the tests highlighted distractibility, impulsiveness and an exaggerated stimulus-bound behaviour (e.g., he could not stop using task-irrelevant objects within his immediate reach, like a pencil even if not needed).

Neuropsychological interview

The speech was correct from the syntactic point of view and content, fluent, fast and friendly. However, comprehension was often difficult due to the examinee's tendency to overlap information, which was often taken for granted. Numerous anomias and automatic verbal expressions occurred, produced impulsively, for instance, Mr White did not fol-low the rules of conversation. Sometimes the content was unclear, so it required reformulating or adding more details. Collectively, these behaviours suggest poor theory or mind.

Mr White was able to report accurately the current events of his per-sonal life but not general events (anterograde amnesia). Furthermore, he showed retrograde amnesia of events that preceded the accident by a few months. For instance, he misplaced important political elections as if they happened during his coma, despite occurring several months prior to that.

Mr White was not able to evaluate objectively his physical, psycho-logical and cognitive condition. For example, he was convinced to be able to go back to his office and to carry out his daily activities auton-omously despite his motor and organisational impairments. He also repeated several times that he only came for the visit because of his mother's insistence.

Neuropsychological and psychometric examination

A global cognitive functioning battery was administered as a screen-ing test (ENB-2), in addition to some in-depth tests related to execu-tive functions (Weigl test, verbal intelligence test and a version of the Hayling Sentence Completion test, see Table 9.1).

Table 9.1 Examinee's cognitive performance: raw scores (correct answers or other) and qualitative assessment (Evaluation) based on age and education-matched controls.

Examinee: Mr Peter White	Evaluation Date 02/ 05 / 2016		
	Raw Scores (correct answer)	Cut-off	Evaluation
ENB-2 Cognitive tests			
Digit Span	7/8	5	Above
Prose Memory (Immediate)	12/28	8	Above
Prose Memory (Delayed)	14/28	11	Above
Interference Memory Test-10 s	7/9	6	Above
Interference Memory Test- 30 s	5/9	5	Borderline
Trail Making Test A	28"	45	Above
Trail Making Test B	100"	140	Above
Token Test	5/5	5	Above
Phonemic Fluency Test (average words per minute)	5.6	11	Below
Abstract Thinking	4/6	4	Borderline
Cognitive Estimation	4/5	4	Borderline
Overlapping Figure Test	25	35	Below
Copy drawing	2/2	2	Above
Spontaneous drawing	2/2	2	Above
Clock drawing Test	10/10	8	Above
Other cognitive tests			
Weigl test	7/15	7	Borderline
Verbal intelligence (proverbs)	19/60	33	Below
Hayling sentence completion A	14/14	14	Above
Other measures			
Cognitive Reserve Index Questionnaire (CRIq) CRI-TOTAL	114	85–114 Average range	within average range
CRI-Education	95		
CRI-Working Activity	106		
CRI-Leisure Time	131		

Legend: relevant scores and evaluations in bold
CUT-OFF = threshold at 5%ile of the normative data
Above = the performance is above cut-off relative to age and education-matched controls.
Below = performance is below cut-off relative to age and education-matched controls
Borderline= performance at the cut-off level relative to age and education-matched controls

Test reference:

ENB-2: Brief Neuropsychological Examination 2nd version (Esame Neuropsicologico Breve 2)
CRIq: Cognitive Reserve questionnaire (Nucci, Mapelli, & Mondini, 2012); http://cri.psy. unipd.it.
Weigl test: normative data in Spinnler & Tognoni (1987)
Verbal intelligence (proverbs): normative data in Splinnler & Tognoni (1987)
Hayling test: Borella et al. (2007)

The results of these tests revealed:

- Impaired performance in memory task: although immediate Prose memory (from ENB-2) was relatively accurate, the delayed version revealed failure to integrate new information with that already remembered. Moreover, during a memory exercise with an interfering task (Interference Memory), the examinee showed difficulties in inhibiting the previous response and showed consequent perseverations. Phonemic incidental memory was also severely impaired, with out-of-context intrusions, for example, Mr White reported names of vegetables when expected to say only animal' names, and repeated the same incorrect answers multiple times. These errors suggest that Mr White's memory impairments are likely underlined by dysexecutive deficits rather than being due to issues with memory per se.
- impaired performance in executive function tasks: impulsivity, for instance, Mr White did not wait for the instructions to be fully delivered (e.g., in TMT-A test), difficulty in inhibiting task-irrelevant information (e.g., in Hayling B), rigidity in abstraction with both verbal and non-verbal material, in reasoning and thinking (verbal intelligence test). For example, he grasped only the concrete or less salient features of stimuli, such as in the case of meaning of proverbs which he paraphrased by missing their abstract meaning. The Cognitive Estimation test (ENB-2) indicated that general knowledge was preserved, although incorrect answers were often given, due to the examinee's impulsive tendency.
- Impaired performance in visual recognition tasks: in the Overlapping figures task, the recognition per se was adequate. However, the many repetitions due to difficulties in inhibiting the stimuli previously selected or recognised and no longer relevant resulted in an overall performance being below average.

Interview with the caregiver (Mother):

After a lively discussion with her son at the beginning of the neuropsychological visit, she reported that her son was not able to organise his working day and tasks and that he does not seem to be aware of his difficulties.

Neuropsychological diagnosis

The cognitive profile that emerged from the neuropsychological assessment revealed the presence of significant difficulties in cognitive control and executive functions. These difficulties emerged particularly in terms of problems in inhibiting an automatic or previously selected response, perseveration errors, difficulty in monitoring his own performance, in abstraction and logic both with verbal and non-verbal material. All these symptoms and signs are compatible with post-traumatic dysexecutive syndrome.

The rehabilitation plan should therefore aim to help the examinee to better control his own behaviour and to improve executive functioning as well as metacognition and awareness.

9.2 A case of initial cognitive decline: in-person setting with paper-and-pencil and digital tests (Setting A)

This case aims to highlight the importance of using different types of test as part of the neuropsychological assessment to disambiguate an uncertain diagnosis. An initial assessment based on traditional paper-and-pencil tests was subsequently complemented by progressively more specific paper-and-pencil as well as digital psychometric tests (see setting A, section 1.3.1).

9.2.1 Information used by the neuropsychologist for the diagnosis

9.2.1.1 Case description

Mr Rossi is a 61-year-old man. He has been living abroad with his wife for many years and has two daughters who live in Italy. He graduated from technical school and then worked for 30 years both in Italy and abroad in a large international company, one of the world's largest in the financial sector.

He first came to the neuropsychology clinic on the recommendation of the geriatrician. At the geriatric examination, Mr Rossi reports having memory problems for a couple of years: he forgets recent events, he defines himself as "absolutely unreliable", he has difficulty in performing fairly simple operations (e.g., getting money from a cash-point), and his wife says that "he has changed". For these reasons, he consulted a neurologist about three years ago and underwent a number of investigations (neuropsychological assessment, neuroimaging tests (PET-FDG), and blood tests). This concluded that there was evidence of a depressive syndrome and since then the examinee has been treated with antidepressants, which, however, have not yielded significant results. Over time, he became increasingly repetitive and mnesic disturbances increased. Both Mr Rossi and his wife claimed that the depressive symptoms had never really occurred.

The geriatrician, therefore, recommended a neuropsychological assessment and further neuroimaging tests (PET-CT and PET with Florbetapir), as the hypothesis of a cortical degenerative disease was raised.

9.2.1.2 Information for the neuropsychological anamnesis

Mr Rossi arrived accompanied by his wife and daughter for the neuropsychological examination. During the neuropsychological interview, the examinee responded passively to the examiner's requests, and he seemed very detached. He reported that he had always led a healthy and active lifestyle, walked a lot, had a passion for cycling, used the computer and has always read a lot. The CRIq (Cognitive Reserve Index questionnaire, Nucci et al., 2012) was administered, a questionnaire that provides an index of cognitive reserve. The CR (Cognitive Reserve) level was 134 which is considered very high relative to the average score of the population (85–114).

The first psychometric assessments based on a fixed-battery led to inconsistent results. Initially, a standard fixed-battery of psychometric tests was administered to assess different aspects of the examinee's cognitive functioning. This first psychometric assessments led to inconclusive results. This might be because a standard battery rather than ad-hoc set of tests was used, following a standard procedure in absence of an established diagnosis. The examinee was therfore further evaluated in a second assessment with computerized tests tailored on this specific examinee.

9.2.1.3 Information from the caregiver

Subsequently, a family member (the examinee's wife) was interviewed. She reported a number of inappropriate behaviours that had recently occurred in the husband's daily life, and in particular his decision to choose early retirement because of underperforming at work.

9.2.2 Chronological step-by-step diagnostic procedure

The assessment aimed to clarify the nature and to quantify the examinee's memory difficulties, and to ascertain their compatibility with a possible cognitive decline.

The diagnostic reasoning will identify any inconsistencies in the examinee's cognitive profile and proceed to make further assessments to clarify them up to when a diagnosis can be formulated.

- *Conclusion from the first examination*: Despite the presence of some mnestic difficulties, the neuropsychological diagnosis at the end of the first assessment (see report) showed an about average cognitive profile when considering age and education. However, the possibility that the high cognitive reserve has "protected" the examinee's cognitive difficulties was raised.

- *Second examination*: A month later, an in-depth assessment with ad hoc-tests instead of a standard battery was requested. This was to investigate the examinee's functioning of mnestic abilities with a gold-standard test for memory and learning, the Free and Cued Selective Reminding Tests (FCSRT, Grober 1987). Additionally, a digital (computerized) test taken from the Vienna Test System (www.schuhfried.at) was used to assess executive functions. In the FCSRT test the examinee's performance was strikingly below average, with difficulties emerging in naming, in semantic associations during the encoding phase and in immediate retrieval. There were also numerous intrusions. Executive functioning was poor, for instance when required to process more than one piece of information simultaneously. In view of the difficulties in memory, learning and executive functions, the neuropsychological diagnosis suggested an early-stage neurodegenerative disease, confirming the hypothesis raised at the first consultation. This was later corroborated by the examionee's results of the PET scan with Florbetapir. It was therefore decided to start pharmacological treatment with anticholinesterase drugs.

- *Third examination*: About six months later, Mr Rossi returned to the neuropsychology outpatient clinic to have a follow-up neuropsychological assessment (with referral to the geriatrician). At this stage, the same tests of the first assessment were administered again. The profile that emerged shows a slight improvement in all the tests administered. Despite the lack of thresholds for significant change, these results are interpreted as a good control of the clinical symptoms (also confirmed by his wife).

It was therefore suggested that Mr Rossi should undergo cognitive stimulation training.

9.2.3 Reports of the three neuropsychological assessments

9.2.3.1 First neuropsychological report

Personal data

Mr Rossi, DoB: 01.01.1960 (61 years old), Male, right-handed
    Address: ...
    Married, living with his wife
    GP: Dr X

Examination context

Date and time: Clinic, 02/05/2021, 2:00 PM
  Place: …
  Who performed the examination: Dr X, neuropsychologist
  Reason and source of referral: geriatrician requiring further diagnostic investigation.
  How an examinee got to the appointment: arrived accompanied by his wife, but was alone during the examination. At the end of the visit, his wife was interviewed.

Available documentation

Geriatric assessment (Dr. X) and PET-FDG (Dr. White). Results were above clinical cut-off.

Neuropsychological anamnesis

Medical history: glaucoma; short syncopal episode after a small dose of beta-blocker. Two years ago, reported memory impairments for recent events and difficulty in performing very familiar actions (e.g., getting money from a cash-point). He was first assessed abroad, and diagnosed with depression; however, both Mr Rossi and his wife disagreed with the diagnosis.
  Pharmacological treatment: Anti-depressant (with no positive results), anti-anxiety.
  Psychological history: No specific events to report. Mr Rossi had good family support, he lives with his wife and has two daughters.
  Cognitive history: Education at university level in informatics engineering (18 years). Fluent in two languages (English and Italian). He loves sports, gardening, DIY, and socialising. He has worked abroad for 30 years in a large internationally well-known company. The cognitive reserve assessed with CRIq was of a very high level (137) because of the stimulating activities he always carried out in his free time (population average at CRIq 85-114, Nucci et al., 2011; http://cri.psy.unipd. it). Currently in early retirement.
  Life habits: good appetite and regular sleeping pattern.
  Mood and behaviour: Adequate and stable during the assessment, with a tendency towards negative mood. Helpful and cooperative, but very passive with respect to prompts from the neuropsychologist. He claimed that there are no difficulties except for some memory disorders. However, during the visit, he acknowledged memory difficulties that he attributed to external factors.

Neuropsychological Interview

The examinee's responses during the interview were adequate and correct in terms of syntax and content. No cognitive difficulties were detected, with the exception of a few anomias and a few circumlocutions. At times the examinee seemed aware of his difficulties (e.g., a sentence in the MMSE is "What is happening to me"). He reported that his main problem was in terms of remembering but, more generally, he felt a sense of uneasiness that he found difficult to accept. On the whole, he alternated moments of denial with others of awareness of his difficulties.

Neuropsychological and psychometric examination

A standard paper-and-pencil test battery was administered (see attached table).

Interview with the caregiver (wife)

Since 2010 she noticed that her husband has been forgetful and that this had increased recently, for instance, he had a tendency to be very repetitive and to forget recent events. She also mentioned that her husband behaved oddly, for instance, he lost interest in his appearance and was confused about the dress code, which was very much unlike him in the past. These problems have also emerged in his working life, which has been less engaging in recent times despite having always been very successful. The wife also noted the husband's tendency to justify his difficulties or mistakes.

Neuropsychological diagnosis

The profile that emerged from the neuropsychological assessment revealed the presence of cognitive difficulties related to memory. These were on the whole within the normal range and possibly masked by Mr Rossi's high cognitive reserve.

Overall, the picture may be compatible with an initial age-related cognitive decline, based on the psychometric results, the qualitative observations during the assessment, and the information from the family member. However, there was a marked discrepancy between Mr Rossi's well-maintained cognitive appearance and the partially declined cognitive performance from psychometric tests.

To clarify this inconsistency and to allow the collection of further data including neuroimaging ones, we, therefore, recommend

Table 9.2 Examinee's cognitive performance in the first assessment: raw scores and qualitative assessment based on age and education-matched controls

Examinee: *Mr Bob Rossi*	*First evaluation 02/ 05 / 2021*		
Tests	*Raw scores*	*Cut-off*	*Evaluation*
Dementia tests			
MMSE	23/30	24	Below
ADAScog	14.3	14-17	Borderline
Cognitive tests	**R.S.**	**S.S.**	**E.S.**
Prose Memory	10.5/28	9.5	1	Borderline
Raven Matrices	30/36	30.5	3	Above
Rey Figure (Copy)	36/36	36.25	4	Above
Rey Figure (Memory)	4.5/36	3.9	0	Below
Phonemic Fluency Test	29	28	4	Above
Semantic Fluency Test	41	41	3	Above
Object Naming (Bada)	29/30			Above
Action Naming (Bada)	26/28			Above
Token Test	35/36		4	Above
Trail Making Test A	41"	32"	4	Above
Trail Making Test B	95"	69"	4	Above
Trail Making Test B-A	54"	44"	4	Above
15 Words Ray Test (Immediate)	31/75	30.6	3	Above
15-words Ray Test (Delayed)	3/15	3	0	Below
Action Imitation	70/72			Above
Wisconsin Card Sorting Test	31	26.9	4	Above
Other measures			
Cognitive Reserve Index		85-114	
Questionnaire (CRIq)	137	Average range	Upper
CRI-TOTAL			Average
CRI-Education	107		
CRI-Working Activity	131		
CRI-Leisure Time	145		

Legend: relevant scores and evaluations in bold
CUT-OFF = threshold at 5th percentile of the normative data
Above = the performance is above 5th percentile relative to age and education-matched controls.
Below = performance is below 5th percentile relative to age and education-matched controls
Borderline = performance at the cut-off level relative to age and education-matched controls
RS = raw score
SS = scaled score
ES = equivalent score
Test reference:
MMSE: Italian normative data in Measso et al., 1993.
ADAScog: normative data in Rosen et al. (1984).
Memory recall test: normative data in Novelli et al. (1986).
Raven Matrices: normative data in Basso, Capitani & Laiacona (1987).
Rey Figura: normative data in Caffarra et al. (2002).
Phonemic and semantic fluency: normative data in Novelli et al. (1986).
Object and action namering (BADA): normative data in Miceli et al. (1994).
Phonemic and Semantic Fluency Test: normative data in Spinnler & Tognoni (1987).
Trail making Test: normative data in Giovagnoli et al. (1996).
15-words Rey Test: normative data in Carlesimo et al. (1995).
Action imitation: normative data in De Renzi et al. (1980).
Wisconsin Card Sorting Test: normative data in Laiacona et al. (2000).
CRIq: Nucci, Mapelli, Mondini (2012); http://cri.psy.unipd.it.

that further, more focused investigations should be carried out in one month.

Best regards

Dr X, neuropsychologist

9.2.3.2 Second neuropsychological report

Personal data

Mr Rossi, DoB: 01.01.1960 (61 years old), Male, right-handed
Address: ...
Married, living with his wife
GP: Dr X

Examination context

Date and time: Clinic, 02/06/2021, 2:00 PM
Place: ...
Who performed the examination: Dr X, neuropsychologist
Reason and source of referral: ad-hoc neuropsychological investigation.
How an examinee got to the appointment: arrived accompanied by his wife, but was alone during the examination. At the end of the visit, his wife was interviewed.

Available documentation

- Previous neuropsychological assessment (Dr X) suggesting a possible initial cognitive decline; please see first neuropsychological assessment.
- Geriatric assessment (Dr. X) with the hypothesis of a cortical degenerative disease;
- PET-FDG resulted normal (Dr. X).
- Interview with the wife.

Neuropsychological anamnesis

See previous report of 02/05/2021 for information regarding the neuropsychological anamnesis.

Mood and behaviour

Compared to the previous examination, the examinee was much more responsive and participated in the examination. He was worried about the diagnosis and was determined to get better and to understand the

144 Examples of clinical cases and reports

reasons for his problems. He reported that in complex and cognitively demanding situations he struggled to maintain concentration. This was confirmed by his performance in today's tests.

Neuropsychological interview

Mr Rossi's responses during the interview were adequate and correct in terms of syntax and content.

Neuropsychological and psychometric examination

A specific in-depth paper-and-pencil and computerised test battery was administered (see attached table). In particular, the 'Free and Cued Selective Reminding Test' (FCSRT), the computerised tests from 'VIenna System Test' (VST) and the 'Brief Neuropsychological Exam' (ENB2) were administered. The computerised tests increased the task's demand and difficulty to allow any impairment to emerge, for instance by reducing the presentation time of the stimuli, or by increasing their visual complexity.

Performance in some paper and pencil tests was average (Digit span and Memory with Interference tests). However, in the FCSRT, the examinee made some simple errors both in naming and in semantic associations, which appeared also in the cued recall.

Deficits in executive functions also emerged (i.e., the Overlapping Figures Test and the Phonemic Fluency Test).

He performed the computerised tests adequately, showing a good capacity of comprehension and retention of information, and maintained working memory processing. However, he failed more demanding tasks, such as those requiring to hold in memory two pieces of information at the same time. In such tasks, the examinee sometimes also forgot the task's instructions.

Interview with the caregiver (wife)

Mr Rossi's wife confirmed the information previously provided and added that since the last visit, her husband seemed more proactive and concerned about his condition.

Neuropsychological diagnosis

The profile that emerged from the neuropsychological assessment revealed the presence of significant difficulties in memory and learning

Table 9.3 Examinee's cognitive performance in the second assessment: raw scores and qualitative assessment based on age and education-matched controls

Examinee: Mr Bob Rossi	Second evaluation 02/ 06 / 2021		
Tests	*Raw Scores*	*Cut-off*	*Evaluation*
ENB-2 e Other tests			
Digit span	6/8	5	Above
Interference Memory Test-10 s	5/9	3	Above
Interference Memory Test- 30 s	6/9	3	Below
Phonemic Fluency Test	5.3	8	Below
Overlapping Figure Test	23	27	Below
FCSRT			
IFR (Immediate Free Recall)	19	19.59	Below
ITR (Immediate Total Recall)	32	<35	Below
DFR (Delayed Free Recall)	7	6.31	Borderline
DTR (Delayed Total Recall)	11	<11	Above
ISC (Index of Sensitivity of Cueing	0.76	<0.9	Below
Number of intrusions	6	>0	Below
VIENNA TEST SYSTEM		PR	
WAFG perceptual & attentive function			
UNIMODAL	PR 2	<16	Below
CROSSMODAL	test interrupted		Below
Stroop (reading)	PR 34	<16	Below
Stroop (naming)	PR 46	<16	Below
NBV-verbal Nback (errors)	PR 18	<16	Borderline

Legend: relevant scores and evaluations in bold
CUT-OFF = threshold at 5%ile of the normative data
PR = percentile rank equivalent to the 16th%ile threshold of the normative data
Above = performance above cut-off relative to age and education-matched controls.
Below = performance below cut-off relative to age and education-matched controls
Borderline = performance at the cut-off level relative to age and education-matched controls
Test reference
ENB-2: normative data in Mondini et al., 2011.
FCSRT: normative data in Grober 1987.
CRIq: Nucci et al., 2011 (http://cri.psy.unipd.it).
Vienna Test System: www.schuhfried.at

as well as in executive and control functions, especially in demanding tasks.

These results confirmed the previous hypothesis of a degenerative disease in its early stage. A 6-month follow-up is recommended to monitor the progression of the condition and assess the efficacy of the medication.

Best regards

Dr X, neuropsychologist

9.2.3.3 Third neuropsychological report

Personal data

Mr Rossi, DoB: 01.01.1960 (61 years old), Male, right-handed
Address: …
Married, living with his wife
GP: Dr X

Examination context

Date and time: Clinic, 02/12/2021, 2:00 PM
Place: …
Who performed the examination: Dr X, neuropsychologist
Reason and source of referral: follow-up neuropsychological investigation.
How an examinee got to the appointment: The examinee arrived accompanied by his wife, but was alone during the examination. At the end of the visit, his wife was interviewed.

Available documentation

- Previous neuropsychological assessment (Dr. X) suggesting a possible initial cognitive decline; please see first neuropsychological assessment.
- Geriatric assessment (Dr. X) with the hypothesis of a cortical degenerative disease;
- PET-FDG resulted normal (Dr. X).
- Interview with the examinee's wife.

Neuropsychological anamnesis

See previous report of 02/05/2021 for information regarding the neuropsychological anamnesis.

Mood and behaviour

The examinee was pleasant and cooperative. A substantial weight loss (6kg) was noticeable.

Neuropsychological interview

The examinee's responses during the interview were adequate and correct in terms of syntax and content.

Neuropsychological and psychometric examination

The same paper-and-pencil as well as computerised tests used in the previous examination were employed for the current assessment (see table 9.4).

Good performance in tests of working memory and of switching attention.

Interview with the caregiver (wife)

Mr. Rossi's wife confirmed the information previously provided. She added that the husband has been highly motivated to carry out the cognitive intervention and was less concerned about his symptoms.

Neuropsychological diagnosis

The profile that emerged from the neuropsychological assessment showed a slight improvement in all the paper-and-pencil and computerised tests administered.

This was likely to reflect the effect of the medication as well as the cognitive rehabilitation treatment, which overall indicated a good control of clinical symptoms.

Best regards

Dr X, neuropsychologist

Table 9.4 Examinee's cognitive performance: raw scores and qualitative assessment based on age and education-matched controls

Examinee: Mr Bob Rossi	Third Evaluation 02/ 12 / 2021		
Tests	*Raw scores*	*Cut-off*	*Evaluation*
Mini-mental State examination	25/30	24	Borderline
MoCA	19/30	21	Below
ENB-2 e ALTRI Test			
Digit span	5/8	5	Above
Interference Memory Test-10 s	9/9	3	Above
Interference Memory Test- 30 s	9/9	3	Above
Phonemic Fluency Test	7.5	8	Below
Overlapping Figure Test	31	27	Above
Trail Making A (seconds)	34	68	Above
Trail Making B (seconds)	101	200	Above

(Continued)

Table 9.4 Examinee's cognitive performance: raw scores and qualitative assessment based on age and education-matched controls *(Continued)*

Examinee: Mr Bob Rossi	Third Evaluation 02/ 12 / 2021		
Tests	Raw scores	Cut-off	Evaluation
FCSRT			
IFR (Immediate Free Recall)	23.12	19.59	Above
ITR (Immediate Total Recall)	32	<35	Below
DFR (Delayed Free Recall)	NT	6.31	NA
DTR (Delayed Total Recall)	NT	<11	NA
ISC (Index of Sensitivity of Cueing	NT	<0.9	NA
Number of intrusions	3	>0	Below
VIENNA TEST SYSTEM		PR	
WAFG perceptual & attentive function			
Unimodal	PR 37	<16	Above
Crossmodal	NT		NA
Stroop (reading)	PR 34	<16	Above
Stroop (naming)	PR 53	<16	Above
NBV-verbal Nback (errors)	PR 73	<16	Above

Legend: relevant scores and evaluations in bold
CUT-OFF = threshold at 5%ile of the normative data
PR = percentile rank equivalent to the 16th%ile threshold of the normative data
Above = performance above clinical cut-off relative to age and education-matched controls.
Below = performance below clinical cut-off relative to age and education-matched controls
Borderline = performance at the clinical cut-off relative to age and education-matched controls
NT = not tested
NA = not available
Test reference
MMSE: normative data in Magni et al., 1996.
ENB-2: normative data in Mondini et al., 2011.
FCSRT: normative data in Grober 1987.
CRIq: Nucci et al., 2011 (http://cri.psy.unipd.it).
MoCA (score estimated from MMSE, Roalf et al., 2012).
Vienna Test System: www.schuhfried.at

9.3 A follow up assessment after brain surgery: remote setting with paper and pencil tests (Setting B)

This case presents a follow-up assessment via video call of an outpatient (Ms Brown) who recently underwent a brain surgery following a right hemisphere tumour.

The assessment based on setting B (section 1.3.2) aimed to examine any long-term consequences of the surgery at a cognitive level. The examinee's well-preserved cognitive functioning immediately following the operation, and the fact that she lived far from the hospital, were ideal factors to favour this remote video-call setting for follow-up testing.

In setting B, the interaction with the neuropsychologist is mostly verbal, with an important key role of their voice which helps engage with the examinee and detect linguistic features of the examinee's speech.

9.3.1 Information used by the neuropsychologist for the assessment

9.3.1.1 Case description

Ms Susan Brown is a left-handed 25-year-old woman with 19 years of education (university degree) currently living with her family and working as a trainee in a business company. In November 2016 she received a medical diagnosis of right-hemisphere glioma (i.e., a brain tumor which begins in the glial cells). The malignancy of the tumor, according to the World Health Organization (WHO) grading system, was judged as low-grade. Low-grade gliomas are slow-growing tumours which can cause a wide range of cognitive deficits. One month after the diagnosis (December 2016) she underwent brain surgery for tumor resection, the mainstay of glioma treatment.

Information for the neuropsychological anamnesis

Before the surgery, Ms Brown's cognitive functioning was evaluated in-person with a detailed neuropsychological screening (MoCA); her cognitive reserve was evaluated with the CRIq (Cognitive Reserve Index questionnaire, Nucci et al., 2012).

Her cognitive functioning was unimpaired, and the CRIq score was average.

Upon re-assessment immediately after the surgery, Ms Brown was alerted and oriented in time and space, her cognitive functioning continued to be unimpaired, and she was feeling well. The only exception was her speech which was qualitatively rather slow but accurate in word selection. Given the successful clinical recovery and the neuropsychological profile, Ms Brown was discharged from hospital.

A routine two-month post-surgery neuropsychological follow-up via video-call took place remotely because of the distance of her home from the hospital.

9.3.2 Chronological step–by–step diagnostic procedure

The follow-up assessment aimed to confirm that Susan's cognitive functioning continued to be maintained following the operation. In particular, rather than a completely self-administered assessment (setting C, section 1.3.3), the neuropsychological investigation was based on a video call with the neuropsychologist (setting B, section 1.3.2) who aimed to evaluate Ms Brown's spontaneous speech since this was slow and hesitant immediately following the operation. The follow-up video call also aimed to understand the origin of Ms Brown's complaints about fatigue in order to be able to suggest a treatment.

The remote follow-up assessment started with the clinical interview. Given that Ms Brow's cognitive abilities were well-preserved following the surgery, the follow-up was only based on a short test. It was reasoned that if performance was unimpaired in this screening test, cognitive functioning would therefore continue to be maintained, whereas any impairment could be examined with further testing.

The screening test used was the MoCA-blind, a tool consisting of auditory stimuli only, currently available for remote settings and adapted from the MoCA. Also here no threshold for significant change were present and so the clinical cut-off was used.

9.3.3 Report of the follow-up neuropsychological assessment

Personal data

Ms Susan Brown, DoB: 11/05/1992 (25 years old), woman, left-handed;
    Address: ...
    Single, living with her family
    GP: Dr X

Examination context

Date and time: 10/12/2017, 9:00 AM.
    Place: Ms Brown's house.
    Who performs the examination: Dr X, neuropsychologist
    Reason and source of referral: To confirm that Ms Brown's cognitive functioning continued to be maintained following the operation, and to understand the origin of her complaints about fatigue in order to be able to suggest a treatment.
    How the examinee dealt with the appointment: Ms Brown was fully independent to deal with the technological aspects of the video call and required no external help throughout the examination, and was fully co-operative.

Available documentation

Medical record including neuroimaging reports (CT scan reporting a massive lesion involving right temporal and parietal lobes).

Neuropsychological anamnesis

Medical history: No specific events to report previous to the tumor.

Pharmacological treatment: Anti-epilectic medication.

Psychological history: No specific events to report. Ms Brown lives with her family and has full family support, the mother being the main carer.

Cognitive history: Education up to degree-level (19 years). The CRIq (Cognitive Reserve Index questionnaire, Nucci et al., 2012) level was 102 which is within average.

(corresponding to a score between 85-114).

Life habits: good appetite and regular sleeping pattern.

Mood and behaviour

From the video-call, Ms Brown's behaviour appeared adequate and stable throughout the assessment.

Neuropsychological interview

In the clinical interview at the start of the remote follow-up assessment, Susan described her cognitive abilities as unimpaired, but she complained about a consistent tiredness which delayed resuming her training in the business company.

In the video call, the neuropsychologist was able to conclude that the speech was correct in terms of syntax and content, it was fluent, and no longer slow compared to the in-patient assessment. The video-call also allowed the neuropsychologist to interact directly with Ms Brown in order to evaluate her fluency and her latency when answering unexpected questions.

Ms Brown was very accurate in reporting current events of her personal life as well as general events. Ms Brown was able to objectively evaluate her physical, psychological and cognitive condition. For example, she knew that she was due to go back to her training, but that this was challenging due to her tiredness.

Neuropsychological and psychometric examination

Cognitive functioning was assessed through the screening test MoCA-Blind. Ms Brown performed all items correctly, as expected from a healthy young person. Ms Brown's maintained performance also included sentence repetition which reflected recovered language abilities. Since the results of the follow-up suggested maintained cognitive functioning (here it was assumed that even without thresholds for

Table 9.5 Examinee's cognitive performance: raw scores (correct answers) in the three assessments

Examinee: Ms Susan Brown	Raw scores (correct answer)		
	Time 1 (Nov 2016): Pre-surgery	Time 2 (Dec 2016): Post-surgery	Time 3 (Feb 2017): Follow up*
MoCA (Montreal Cognitive Assessment)			
Visuo-spatial executive	5/5	5/5	NA
Naming	3/3	3/3	NA
Attention (digit)	2/2	2/2	2/2
Attention (reading letters)	1/1	1/1	1/1
Attention (calculation)	3/3	3/3	3/3
Language (repetition)	2/2	2/2	2/2
Language (Fluency)	1/1	1/1	1/1
Abstraction	2/2	2/2	2/2
Delayed recall	4/5	5/5	5/5
Orientation	6/6	5/6	6/6
Total score	29/30	29/30	22/22
Other measures			
Cognitive Reserve Index Questionnaire (CRIq) CRI-TOTAL	102	NT	NT
CRI-Education	103		
CRI-Working Activity	102		
CRI-Leisure Time	110		

Legend: relevant scores and evaluations in bold
NA= not available; NT= not tested
Test reference:
MoCA: Montreal Cognitive Assessment (Nassreddine et al., 2005),
*MoCa Blind version which has no visuo-spatial executive and naming tests (max score=22)
CRIq: Cognitive Reserve questionnaire (Nucci et al., 2012); http://cri.psy.unipd.it

significant change the information was sufficient), no further testing was required (see Table 9.5).

Interview with the caregiver

Ms Brown's mother was interviewed the day after the follow-up assessment to gather her description of the daughter's condition. She confirmed Ms Brown's preserved cognitive functioning but mentioned the lack of energy and fatigue. For instance, she reported Ms Brown's intention to continue resting at home before returning to her previous activity in the business company.

Neuropsychological diagnosis

The cognitive profile that emerged from the follow-up assessment revealed maintained cognitive functioning. The initial slowness in Ms Brown's spontaneous speech appeared to be fully recovered in the follow up session.

Ms Brown's self-reported chronic tiredness was still persistent at the follow-up stage and was therefore due to be further discussed with the medical team.

9.4 The case of a healthy older woman: remote setting with self-administered tests (Setting C)

The following case aims to highlight how setting C could be suitable to monitor a potential age-related decline. This is the case of a woman who was asked to perform an online test by the neuropsychologist she consulted in order to monitor her cognitive efficiency.

In setting C (section 1.3.3), there is no direct interaction with the neuropsychologist who can either remotely monitor the outcome of the testing, or can subsequently be contacted by the examinee to discuss the results of the assessment.

9.4.1 Case description

Mrs Green is a 77-year-old woman who arriveed alone at the Neuropsychology out-patients' clinic. During a neurological examination, she reported concerns related to concentration and episodic memory; these problems seem to have increased following her retirement from the estate agency family business two years previously. For instance, she mentioned her tendency to forget people or the names of objects.

Mrs Green was living by herself after her husband died. She had obtained her A level qualifications, and reported having attended a university course almost to the end. From the outset, she appeared to be very tense and worried, yet cooperative.

Mrs. Green was sent to a neuropsychologist in order to investigate the nature of her memory complaints. Performance assessed with a short cognitive screening was within the upper limit of the normal range. Therefore, the neuropsychologist's advice to Mrs Green was to carry out regular (monthly) self-administered cognitive screenings to monitor her cognitive performance and detect possible changes.

9.4.2 Neuropsychological step-by-step procedure

Given the uncertain nature of Mrs. Green's memory complaints, a six-month follow-up was planned to further discuss the symptoms and the results of the cognitive screenings. During this six-month period, the neuropsychologist planned to regularly monitor her performance to detect any sudden changes and in turn inform the examinee. A report by the neuropsychologist was due to be written at the end of the six months examination time after an in-person meeting with Mrs. Green to complete data collection.

No neuropsychological diagnosis is provided in setting C.

CHEATSHEET

Principles of the Interpretative Approach

1 The neuropsychologist plays an active role in every aspect of the neuropsychological assessment.

2 The neuropsychological assessment is a rational process of collecting evidence on the cognitive status of an examinee and of drawing a conclusion.

3 In any neuropsychological assessment, the neuropsychologist must integrate and interpret all the available evidence to draw a conclusion.

4 The use of results from neuropsychological tests always implies an active interpretation made by the neuropsychologist.

5 The neuropsychologist should be aware of implicit inferences when interpreting available evidence.

6 A neuropsychological assessment can be considered as such, only when there has been a direct observation (in-person or remote settings) of the examinees' behaviour and a direct interaction with them.

Measurement

Phases of neuropsychological assessment

1 Anamnesis/Interview with the examinee
Collecting data on past and on the present time: 1) medical history 2) psychological history 3) cognitive history

2 Psychometric assessment
   - Tests are selected according to either 1) Fixed battery 2) Flexible approach 3) Mixed approach.
   - Results of tests are always *interpreted* by the neuropsychologist, taking into account all available sources of information (other tests, qualitative observation, test properties as validity and reliability).

3 Interview with the caregivers (if possible)
Collecting further data to corroborate or complement the examinee's report

4 Neuropsychological diagnosis
Diagnosis at three levels: 1) descriptive diagnosis, 2) diagnosis of compatibility with an aetiology, 3) functional diagnosis.

5 Report
Report should include all collected information and also a neuropsychological diagnosis.

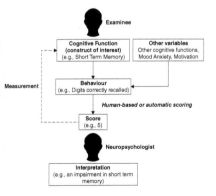

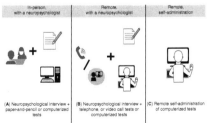

(A) Neuropsychological interview + paper-and-pencil or computerized tests

(B) Neuropsychological interview + telephone, or video call tests or computerized tests

(C) Remote self-administration of computerized tests

Appendix 1: Form used by the neuropsychologist to collect signs and symptoms during an assessment

Signs	Symptoms
Signs observed during the interview	Symptoms reported by the examinee
Signs observed during the psychometric assessment	Symptoms reported by the carer/special one
Signs reported by the carer/special one	

Appendix 2: The Cognitive Reserve Index Questionnaire (CRIq)

This questionnaire is a tool for collecting the examinee's cognitive history and for quantifying their Cognitive Reserve. This includes a global index of cognitive reserve (CRI), which can be broken down into three major areas: education, work activities and leisure activities, corresponding to CRI-Education, CRI-Working activity, and CRI-Leisure time activity. A series of semi-structured questions for each of these sections assesses how often certain activities have been practised and for how many years. The three-part questionnaire was constructed to equally contribute to the Cognitive Reserve Index, by adjusting for age since this strongly correlates with the CRIq (Nucci et al. 2012; see http://cri.psy.unipd.it for the questionnaire and instructions. See also the new edition, shorter and possible also as a self-administered version of the questionnaire available online: www.cognitivereserveindex.org/NewEdition/index.html).

The CRI-Education index simply computes the number of years of formal education or any training courses taken in adulthood. The CRI-Working activity classifies 5 different levels of occupation based on the intellectual effort they require, unskilled, manual work (e.g., farmer, car driver, call centre operator), skilled manual work (e.g., craftsman, clerk, hairdresser), skilled non-manual or technical work (e.g., trader, kindergarten teacher, real estate agent); professional occupation (e.g., lawyer, psychologist, physician), highly intellectual occupation (e.g., university professor, judge, top manager). It records the number of years in each profession over the lifespan of a participant.

Finally, the CRI-Leisure time activity index considers cognitively stimulating activities other than study or work. The selection of the relevant activities was carried out through the Item Response Theory procedure (Rizopoulos, 2006; Van Der Linden & Hambleton, 1997).

The final version with 16 items, presented in a series of semi-structured questions, includes the most relevant in a sample of Italian adults and has a good reliability (α=0.73, 95% CI [0.70, 0.76]).

Appendix 3: Implicit inferences in the report

This appendix reports the same neuropsychological report as in section 9.1. This time, however, all the <u>underlined</u> text highlights the main inferences made by the neuropsychologist, and written in the report. Explanations of the underlined inferences are reported within square brackets, beside the original text [*NPS = neuropsychologist*].

By examining this detailed report, the reader may further appreciate the active role played by the neuropsychologist, and the importance of the inferences made, which may otherwise be unnoticed as they are often implicit. Making inferences is a necessary part of the diagnostic process and is one of the key roles of the neuropsychologist. After reading this enriched report, the reader is invited to go through all the other reports in 9.1 and to identify the sections of the text reflecting inferences made by the neuropsychologist.

Report of the neuropsychological assessment

Personal data

Mr. Peter White, DoB: 21/04/1975 (41 years old), Male, right-handed (currently he cannot move the right arm correctly)
Address: ...
Divorced, living alone
GP: Dr X

Examination context

Reason and source of referral: request from intensive care neurologist to treat the behavioural and cognitive dysfunctional profile following the acute phase of the examinee head trauma.

How the examinee got to the appointment: Mr White was an in-patient who arrived at the examination accompanied by his mother but he was on his own during the neuropsychological examination. He was cooperative throughout.

Available documentation

Medical record including neuroimaging reports (CT scan reporting hypodense areas in the left parietal and temporal regions, as well as bilateral frontal). In the acute phase, cognitive reports indicated the examinee's state of confusion and lack of behavioural inhibition.

Neuropsychological anamnesis

Medical history: No specific events to report.

Pharmacological treatment: Current anti-epilectic medication.

Psychological history: No specific events to report. The examinee lives on his own and has limited family support, the examinee's mother being the main carer.

Cognitive history: Education up to A-level (13 years). The CRIq (Cognitive Reserve Index questionnaire, Nucci et al., 2012) level was 114 which is about average (corresponding to a score between 85–114). Peter's CRIq reflected his leisure's activities rather than his education or work-ing activities. He reported to have an active lifestyle, passion for sports including sensation-seeking activities such as gliding, or speleology.

Life habits: good appetite and regular sleeping pattern.

Mood and behaviour

Adequate and stable during the assessment. There was, however, a certain irritability during the conversation with his mother. At a behavioural level, qualitative observations during the administration of the tests, highlighted distractibility, impulsiveness and an exagger-ated stimulus-bound behaviour (e.g., he could not stop using task-irrelevant objects within his immediate reach, like a pencil even if not needed). [*NPS assumes that this behaviour is indeed clinically relevant in relation to the trauma and the brain areas involved, and it is not only related to anxiety or to personality traits already present before the trauma*]

Neuropsychological interview

The speech was correct from the syntactic point of view and content, fluent, fast and friendly. However, comprehension was often difficult due to the examinee's tendency to overlap information, which was often taken for granted. Numerous anomias and automatic verbal expressions occurred, produced impulsively, for instance Mr White did not follow the rules of conversation. Sometimes the content was unclear, so it required reformulating or adding more details. Collectively, these behaviours suggest poor theory or mind. [*NPS interprets lack of clarity of the content, impulsivity, and the inability to follow basic rules of conversation as possibly related to a single impairment in Theory of Mind*]

Mr White was able to report accurately the current events of his personal life but not general events (anterograde amnesia). [*NPS interprets lack of knowledge as amnesia*]

Furthermore, he showed retrograde amnesia of events that preceded the accident by a few months. [*NPS interprets lack of memory as retrograde amnesia and as clinically relevant*]. For instance, he misplaced important political elections as if they happened during his coma, despite occurring several months prior to that.

Mr White was not able to evaluate objectively his physical, psychological and cognitive condition. For example, he was convinced to be able to go back to his office and to carry out his daily activities autonomously despite his motor and organisational impairments. He also repeated several times that he only came for the visit because of his mother's insistence.

Neuropsychological and psychometric examination

A global cognitive functioning battery was administered as a screening test (ENB-2), in addition to some in-depth tests related to executive functions (Weigl test, verbal intelligence test and a version of the Hayling Sentence Completion test, see Table 9.1).

The results of these tests revealed:

- Impaired performance in memory tasks: although immediate Prose memory (from ENB-2) was relatively accurate, the delayed version revealed failure to integrate new information with that already remembered. Moreover, during a memory exercise with an interfering task (Interference memory), the examinee showed difficulties in inhibiting the previous response and showed consequent perseverations. Phonemic incidental memory was also severely impaired, with out-of-context intrusions, for example, Mr White reported names of vegetables when expected to say only animal' names, and repeated the same incorrect answers multiple times. These errors suggest that Mr White's memory impairments are likely underlined by dysexecutive deficits rather than refecting issues with memory per se. [*The NPS interprets a below cut-off performance in memory tasks by giving importance to the qualitative aspects emerged, and also on the available information from interview and anamnesis, reaching the conclusion that the deficits may be related not to memory, but to an executive disorder*].

• Impaired performance in Executive functions tasks: impulsivity, for instance, Mr White did not wait for the instructions to be fully delivered (e.g., in TMT-A test), difficulty in inhibiting task-irrelevant information (e.g., in Hayling B), rigidity in abstraction with both verbal and non-verbal material, in reasoning and thinking (verbal intelligence test). For example, he grasped only the concrete or less salient features of stimuli, such as in the case of meaning of proverbs which he paraphrased by missing their abstract meaning. Cognitive Estimation test (ENB-2) indicated that general knowledge was preserved, although incorrect answers were often given, due to the examinee's impulsive tendency. [*The NPS interprets some behaviours in light to a general tendency*].

• Impaired performance in Visual recognition tasks: in the Overlapping figures task, the recognition per se was adequate. However, the many repetitions due to difficulties in inhibiting the stimuli previously selected or recognised and no longer relevant resulted in an overall performance being below average. [*The NPS interprets a below-cut-off result in visual recognition; based on qualitative observation, results on other tests and the overall information available, the examinee has not a visual recognition deficit, but rather than impaired performance is related to other issues, and not to the main construct measured by the test, see par 4.3*]

Interview with the caregiver (Mother)

After a lively discussion with her son at the beginning of the neuropsychological visit, she reported that her son was not able to organise his working day and tasks and that he did not seem to be aware of his difficulties.

Neuropsychological diagnosis

The cognitive profile that emerged from the neuropsychological assessment revealed the presence of significant difficulties in cognitive control and executive functions. These difficulties emerged particularly in terms of problems in inhibiting an automatic or previously selected

response, perseveration errors, difficulty in monitoring his own performance, in abstraction and logic both with verbal and non-verbal
material. All these symptoms are compatible with post-traumatic
dysexecutive syndrome

[*The NPS summarises the overall pattern of information, into a coherent
scheme that is compatible with the anamnesis and parsimoniously and with high
probability explains all the signs observed, the symptoms reported, based on an
active integration of all the available information*].

The rehabilitation plan should therefore aim to help the examinee to
better control his own behaviour and to improve executive functioning
as well as metacognition and awareness.

Glossary

Closed questions: These are questions which require one or two words as an answer and are usually related to familiar or personal topics, for example related to the examinee's identity ("What is your name?", "Where do you live?", "When were you born?"). Close questions are especially useful in the initial phase of the interview because examinees are likely to answer them smoothly, therefore facilitating the start of the conversation, avoiding anxiety-provoking questions and demanding cognitive processing. This is especially important in the case of examinees who are fearful, worried or even frightened.

Cognitive assessment: Includes the whole process of collecting and interpreting psychometric data, to identify cognitive impairments or classify cognitive performance. Differently from the 'neuropsychological assessment', the cognitive assessment makes no hypotheses on the etiological causes of the observed performance. The focus is on the description of cognitive performance (e.g., the examinee has language abilities that are worse than average) and not on the underlying cause of the possible impairments (e.g., worse performance is related to an early-life developmental disorder or to a recent neurodegenerative disease).

Condition of interest: Any condition to be detected by a test (typically the presence of a pathology/disease or a cognitive impairment).

Diagnostic reasoning: The diagnostic process that the neuropsychologist carries out during and especially after the examination consisting of integrating all data of the examinee (anamnestic, behavioural and psychometric) in order to obtain a coherent picture of their mental status (descriptive diagnosis) or to find the compatibility of their impairment with an aetiological origin (aetiological diagnosis) or to explain how their impairment affects their daily living currently and in the future (functional diagnosis).

Digital tests (also called computerised tests): Psychometric tests used to evaluate cognitive functioning via digital devices such as computers, tablets, or smartphones. The examinee can answer questions interacting directly with the device, for example using a key-board or tapping on the screen of a tablet.

Interpretation: The act of explaining the meaning of something. In the context of this book, interpretation is associated with assigning a meaning to observable phenomena or to the information collected in the neuropsychological assessment.

Interpretative Approach to neuropsychological assessment: This is the approach presented in this book. It highlights the importance of the neuropsychologist's *interpretations* during the assessment of signs, symptoms and test scores. This approach underlines the active role of the neuropsychologist throughout the assessment. It is based on several principles that guide a rational understanding of the assessment process.

Measurement: The assignment of numerals to objects or events according to rules (Stevens, 1946). Note that there are many possible definitions of measurement (see section 4.3).

Mirroring technique: It is the act of mirroring a verbal behaviour of the examinee, imitating as much as possible their communication style by using the same modality and vocabulary. It is used by the neuropsychologist to *tune in* with an examinee in order to understand their mood and to facilitate the neuropsychological evaluation. For example, a neuropsychologist may repeat a specific adjective or word used by the examinee (see examples in the text for more details).

Neuropsychological assessment/Neuropsychological evaluation: Includes the whole process of collecting and interpreting anamnestic information, data from the neuropsychological interview and psychometric data, in order to reach a neuropsychological diagnosis.

Neuropsychological diagnosis: The final product of the whole process of collecting and integrating information and data about the examinee. A neuropsychological diagnosis can be made at three different levels: 1. Descriptive, which provides an overview of the spared and impared cognitive functions; 2. Diagnosis of compatibility with an Aetiology, in which a cognitive profile matches a possible underlying medical diagnosis; and 3. Functional, based on information collected in the descriptive and aetiological diagnosis, and formulated only after them. It provides a prognosis, including a possible rehabilitation plan, or a judgement of the level of independence of an examinee (e.g., in relation to their ability to live independently, or to continue working or going to school). It depends on a number of factors such as the examinee's age, civil and socio-economic status.

Neuropsychological interview: The initial verbal interaction and communication between the neuropsychologist and an examinee. The interview has different purposes such as collecting information from the examinee about their daily living, their past experiences and their symptoms, but also to detect their ability to communicate and their spontaneous speech. It also poses the fundations to the relationship between the neuropsychologist and the examinee, which is important for the neuropsychological assessment.

Neuropsychological setting: The physical environment in which a neuropsychological assessment takes place, and also the relationship between a neuropsychologist and an examinee, which can influence the outcome of the evaluation. There are at least three types of neuropsychological settings: setting A, in person with paper and pencil tests or digital tests; setting B, remote, by telephone or videocall; setting C, self administration of digital tests.

Neuropsychological test: A psychometric test used during the neuropsychological assessment. Typically, a neuropsychological test is a *performance-based* test measuring a specific cognitive function (or some properties of the cognitive function), but it can also measure other constructs, or have other uses (see Chapter 4). Neuropsychological tests can be in paper-and-pencil or digital format.

Non-verbal features of the behaviour of the examinee: Part of the meta-communication aspects of posture and body movements, hand movements, eye contact and facial expressions.

Open questions: With no predictable answers, these questions allow the examinee to speak freely and independently. They offer the neuropsychologist an opportunity to analyse the examinee's spontaneous speech especially in terms of the organisation of the content of the conversation and its delivery, and to detect technical errors like the presence of anomias, paraphasias, latencies, circumlocutions, etc.

Paper-and-pencil test: Traditional psychometric tests used to evaluate cognitive functioning based on verbally- and visually-presented material, such as pictures to name, to draw or to categorise or wooden blocks to arrange.

Paraverbal features of the behaviour of the examinee: Features in the speech of the examinee that are related to the metacommunicative level, such as rhythm, voice volume, prosody, pauses among words or sentences.

Pathognomonic signs: Clinical features reflecting a specific neuropsychological disorder.

Psychometric assessment: The part of the assessment specifically involving the administration of psychometric tests following a precise procedure and resulting in one or more scores for each test.

Psychometric test: A psychological test involving measurement. Neuropsychological tests are a specific type of psychometric tests.

Reformulating technique: Consists of rewording what the examinee said to ensure that the neuropsychologist understands the message they intend to communicate and to demonstrate good listening.

Reliability: The extent to which a test consistently provides a measure. In particular, a test is reliable if it provides consistent results across time, or across raters or users.

Sensitivity: The property of a test to detect true positive results (see Chapter 8). In neuropsychology, this corresponds to correctly identifying a *condition of interest* (typically a disease) when it is effectively present.

Specificity: The property of a test to detect true negative results. In neuropsychology, this corresponds to correctly identifying the absence of a *condition of interest* (so, the absence of a disease). Hence, most of the time specificity in neuropsychological tests refers to identifying healthy controls or maintained performance.

Test interpretation: The process of drawing a conclusion on the basis of the results of a test. It implies making an inference about factors that underlie the performance.

Two-forced choice questions: Here there are usually two possible alternative answers for the examinee to choose from. These questions aim to facilitate and encourage the examinee's verbal production, especially when an examinee is not very talkative or when there is a clear language impairment that may hamper the communication. Two-forced choice questions can substitute open questions. For instance, instead of asking: "What do you do during the day?" it may be possible to say: "Do you usually stay in or go out during the day?", or "Do you watch television or do you read newspapers?". Questions should be short and clearly expressed, with no more than two alternative answers, such that they are not influenced by memory or language difficulties.

Validity: The property of a tool to measure the construct it actually aims to measure.

Verbal features of the behaviour of the examinee: The lexical selection, the syntactical and morphological structure of the language production in the examinee's speech. Verbal features also include errors like anomias, anomic latencies, paraphasias (phonemic or semantic) and phonetic distortions.

Bibliography

Abbate, C., & Trimarchi, P. D. (2013). Clinical neuropsychologists need a standard preliminary observational examination of cognitive functions. *Frontiers in Psychology, 4*, 314.

Aiello, E. N., Rimoldi, S., Bolognini, N., Appollonio, I., & Arcara, G. (2021). Psychometrics and diagnostics of Italian cognitive screening tests: A systematic review. *Neurological Sciences*, 1–25.

Angeleri, R., Bosco, F. M., Gabbatore, I., Bara, B. G., & Sacco, K. (2012). Assessment battery for communication (ABaCo): Normative data. *Behavior Research Methods, 44*(3), 845–861.

Arcara, G. et al. (2013). Normative data for the Italian version of the Montreal Cognitive Assessment (MoCA): The impact of sociocultural variables on cut-offs. Poster presentation at the International Neuropsychological Society 2013 Mid-Year Meeting. Amsterdam.

Arcara, G., & Bambini, V. (2016). A test for the Assessment of Pragmatic Abilities and Cognitive Substrates (APACS): Normative data and psychometric properties. *Frontiers in Psychology, 7*(70). doi:10.3389/fpsyg.2016.00070

Arcara, G., Burgio, F., Benavides-Varela, S., Toffano, R., Gindri, P., Tonini, E., ... & Semenza, C. (2017). Numerical activities of daily living–financial (NADL-F): A tool for the assessment of financial capacities. *Neuropsychological Rehabilitation*.

Assem, M., Lando, M., Grissi, M., Kamel, S., Massy, Z. A., Chillon, J. M., & Hénaut, L. (2018). The impact of uremic toxins on cerebrovascular and cognitive disorders. *Toxins, 10*(7), 303.

Azocar, I., Livingston, G., & Huntley, J. (2021, Feb 4). The association between impaired awareness and depression, anxiety, and apathy in mild to moderate Alzheimer's disease: A systematic review. *Front Psychiatry*.

Barletta-Rodolfi, C., Gasparini, F., & Ghidoni, E. (2011). Kit del neuropsicologo italiano. *Bologna: Società Italiana di Neuropsicologia*.

Bastiaanse, R., Raaijmakers, S., Satoer, D., & Visch-Brink, E. (2016). The multilingual Token Test. *Aphasiology, 30*(4), 508–508.

Begolo, M., Gaggi, O., Mondini, S., & Montemurro, S. (2019). Digital neuropsychological assessment of discourse production: An interdisciplinary approach, in EAI International Conference on Smart Objects and Technologies for Social Good (GoodTechs'19), September 25–27, 2019, Valencia, Spain and New York, NY: ACM.

Bell, B. D., & Roper, B. L. (1998). Myths of neuropsychology: Another view. *The Clinical Neuropsychologist*, *12*(2), 237–244.

Benjamini, Y., & Hochberg, Y. (1995). Controlling the false discovery rate: a practical and powerful approach to multiple testing. *Journal of the Royal Statistical Society: Series B (Methodological)*, *57*(1), 289–300.

Benjamini, Y., & Yekutieli, D. (2001). The control of the false discovery rate in multiple testing under dependency. *Annals of Statistics*, 1165–1188.

Bennet, T. L. (2001). Neuropsychological evaluation in rehabilitation planning and evaluation of functional skills. *Archives of Clinical Neuropsychology*, *16*(3), 237–253.

Bilder, R. M., & Reise, S. P. (2019). Neuropsychological tests of the future: How do we get there from here? *The Clinical Neuropsychologist*, *33*(2), 220–245.

Bilder, R. M., Postal, K. S., Barisa, M., Aase, D. M., Cullum, C. M., Gillaspy, S. R., Harder, L., Kanter, G., Lanca, M., Lechuga, D. M., Morgan, J. M., Most, R., Puente, A. E., Salinas, C. M., & Woodhouse, J. (2020). Inter Organizational Practice Committee Recommendations/Guidance for Teleneuropsychology in Response to the COVID-19 Pandemic. *Archives of Clinical Neuropsychology: The official journal of the National Academy of Neuropsychologists*, *35*(6), 647–659.

Bond, T. G., & Fox, C. M. (2007). *Applying the Rasch Model: Fundamental Measurement in the Human Sciences*, 2nd edition. Mahwah, NJ: Lawrence Erlbaum, Associates Publishers.

Borella, E., Carretti, B., & De Beni, R. (2007). *Accertamento della Memoria negli Adulti [The evaluation of memory in adulthood]*. Firenze: Organizzazioni Speciali.

Boringa, J. B., Lazeron, R. H., Reuling, I. E., Ader, H. J., Pfennings, L. E., Lindeboom, J., … & Polman, C. H. (2001). The brief repeatable battery of neuropsychological tests: normative values allow application in multiple sclerosis clinical practice. *Multiple Sclerosis Journal*, *7*(4), 263–267.

Bratsberg, B., & Rogeberg, O. (2018). Flynn effect and its reversal are both environmentally caused. *Proceedings of the National Academy of Sciences*, *115*(26), 6674–6678.

Burgess, P. W., & Shallice, T. (1996). Response suppression, initiation and strategy use following frontal lobe lesions. *Neuropsychologia*, *33*(4), 263–272.

Buyukdura, J. S., McClintock, S. M., & Croarkin, P. E. (2011). Psychomotor retardation in depression: Biological underpinnings, measurement, and treatment. *Progress in Neuro-psychopharmacology & Biological Psychiatry*, *35*(2), 395–409.

Capitani, E. (1997). Normative data and neuropsychological assessment. Common problems in clinical practice and research. *Neuropsychological Rehabilitation*, *7*(4), 295–310. https://doi.org/10.1080/713755543

Capitani, E., & Laiacona, M. (1997). Composite neuropsychological batteries and demographic correction: Standardisation based on equivalent scores, with a review of published data. *Journal of Clinical and Experimental Neuropsychology*, *19*(6), 795–809.

Capitani, E., & Laiacona, M. (1999). The evaluation of experimental data in neuropsychology, in Denes, G., & Pizzamiglio, L., *Handbook of Clinical and Experimental Neuropsychology*. London: Psychology Press.

Casaletto, K. B., & Heaton, R. K. (2017). Neuropsychological assessment: Past and future. *Journal of the International Neuropsychological Society, 23*(9–10), 778–790.

Chaytor, N., & Schmitter-Edgecombe, M. (2003). The ecological validity of neuropsychological tests: A review of the literature on everyday cognitive skills. *Neuropsychology Review, 13*(4), 181–197.

Cherner, M., Marquine, M. J., Umlauf, A., Morlett Paredes, A., Rivera Mindt, M., Suárez, P., ... & Heaton, R. K. (2021). Neuropsychological norms for the US-Mexico Border Region in Spanish (NP-NUMBRS) project: Methodology and sample characteristics. *The Clinical Neuropsychologist, 35*(2), 253–268.

Cohen, R. A. (1999). Alteration of intention and self-initiated action associated with bilateral anterior cingulotomy. *Journal of Neuropsychiatry and Clinical Neurosciences, 11*(4), 444–453.

Collie, A., Darby, D. G., Falleti, M. G., Silbert, B. S., & Maruff, P. (2002). Determining the extent of cognitive change after coronary surgery: A review of statistical procedures. *The Annals of Thoracic Surgery, 73*(6), 2005–2011.

Conti, S., Bonazzi, S., Laiacona, M., Masina, M., & Coralli, M. V. (2015). Montreal Cognitive Assessment (MoCA)-Italian version: Regression based norms and equivalent scores. *Neurological Sciences, 36*(2), 209–214.

Crawford, J. R., & Howell, D. C. (1998). Comparing an individual's test score against norms derived from small samples. *The Clinical Neuropsychologist, 12*(4), 482–486.

Crawford, J. R., & Garthwaite, P. H. (2006). Comparing patients' predicted test scores from a regression equation with their obtained scores: a significance test and point estimate of abnormality with accompanying confidence limits. *Neuropsychology, 20*(3), 259–271.

Crawford, J. R., Garthwaite, P. H., & Betkowska, K. (2009). Bayes' theorem and diagnostic tests in neuropsychology: interval estimates for post-test probabilities. *The Clinical Neuropsychologist, 23*(4), 624–644.

Crawford, J. R., Garthwaite, P. H., & Porter, S. (2010). Point and interval estimates of effect sizes for the case-controls design in neuropsychology: rationale, methods, implementations, and proposed reporting standards. *Cognitive Neuropsychology, 27*(3), 245–260.

Crawford, J. R., Howell, D. C., & Garthwaite, P. H. (1998). Payne and Jones revisited: estimating the abnormality of test score differences using a modified paired samples t-test. *Journal of Clinical and Experimental Neuropsychology, 20*(6), 898–905.

Critchley, M. (1953). *The Parietal Lobes.* New York: Hafner Publisher.

Cronback, L. J. (1970). *Essentials of Psychological Testing*, 3rd edition. New York: Harper & Row.

De Renzi, E., & Vignolo, L. A. (1962). The Token Test: A sensitive test to detect receptive disturbances in aphasics. *Brain, 85*(4), 665–678.

Delazer, M., Girelli, L., Granà, A., & Domahs, F. (2003). Number processing and calculation: Normative data from healthy adults. *The Clinical Neuropsychologist, 17*(3), 331–350.

Deleau, M. (2012). Language and theory of mind: Why pragmatics matter. *European Journal of Developmental Psychology, 9*(3), 295–312.

Demeyere, N., Riddoch, M. J., Slavkova, E. D., Bickerton, W. L., & Humphreys, G. W. (2015). The Oxford Cognitive Screen (OCS): Validation of a stroke-specific short cognitive screening tool. *Psychological Assessment, 27*(3), 883.

Derksen, F., Bensing, J., & Lagro-Janssen, A. (2013). Effectiveness of empathy in general practice: a systematic review. *British Journal of General Practice, 63*(606), e76–e84.

Dodrill, C. B. (1997). Myths of neuropsychology. *The Clinical Neuropsychologist, 11*(1), 1–17.

Dubois, B., Slachevsky, A., Litvan, I., & Pillon, B. (2000). The FAB: A frontal assessment battery at bedside. *Neurology, 55*(11), 1621–1626.

Dutton, E., van der Linden, D., & Lynn, R. (2016). The negative Flynn Effect: A systematic literature review. *Intelligence, 59,* 163–169.

Fastenau, P. S. (1998). Validity of regression-based norms: An empirical test of the comprehensive norms with older adults. *Journal of Clinical and Experimental Neuropsychology, 20*(6), 906–916.

Feenstra, H., Murre, J., Vermeulen, I. E., Kieffer, J. M., & Schagen, S. B. (2018). Reliability and validity of a self-administered tool for online neuropsychological testing: The Amsterdam Cognition Scan. *Journal of Clinical and Experimental Neuropsychology, 40*(3), 253–273.

Feinkohl, I., Janke, J., & Hadzidiakos, D. et al. (2019). Associations of the metabolic syndrome and its components with cognitive impairment in older adults. *BMC Geriatr., 19,* 77.

Ferrara, K. W. (1994). *Therapeutic Ways with Words.* New York, NY: Oxford University Press.

Flynn, J. R. (1987). Massive IQ gains in 14 nations: What IQ tests really measure. *Psychological Bulletin, 101*(2), 171–191.

Folstein, M. F., Fólstein, S. E., & McHugh, P. R. (1975). Mini-mental state: A practical method for grading the cognitive state of patients for the clinician. *Journal of Psychiatric Research. 12*(3), 189–198.

Formánek, T., Csajbók, Z., Wolfová, K. et al. (2020). Trajectories of depressive symptoms and associated patterns of cognitive decline. *Sci. Rep., 10,* 20888.

Fratiglioni, L., Paillard-Borg, S., & Winblad, B. (2004). An active and socially integrated lifestyle in late life might protect against dementia. *Lancet Neurol., 3*(6), 343–353.

Gelman, A., Hill, J., & Yajima, M. (2012). Why we (usually) don't have to worry about multiple comparisons. *Journal of Research on Educational Effectiveness, 5*(2), 189–211.

Goldberg, E., & Costa, L. D. (1986). Qualitative indices in neuropsychological assessment: An extension of Luria's approach to executive deficit following prefrontal lesions, in Grant, I., & Adams, K. M. (Eds), *Neuropsychological Assessment of Neuropsychiatric Disorders* (pp. 48–64). New York: Oxford University Press.

Goldstein, G. (1997). The clinical utility of standardized or flexible battery approaches to neuropsychological assessment, in Goldstein, G., & Incaglioli, T., *Contemporary Approaches to Neuropsychological Assessment* (pp. 67–91). Cham: Springer.

Goldstein, G., & Incaglioli, T. (1997). *Contemporary Approaches to Neuropsychological Assessment.* New York: Plenum Press.

Goldstein, L. H., & McNeil, J. E. (Eds) (2012). *Clinical Neuropsychology: A Practical Guide to Assessment and Management for Clinicians.* New York: John Wiley & Sons.

Grant, I., & Adams, K. M. (Eds) (1996). *Neuropsychological Assessment of Neuropsychiatric Disorders.* New York: Oxford University Press.

Greher, M. R., & Wodushek, T. R. (2017). Performance validity testing in neuropsychology: Scientific basis and clinical application: A brief review. *Journal of Psychiatric Practice, 23*(2), 134–140.

Greve, K. W., Ord, J., Curtis, K. L., Bianchini, K. J., & Brennan, A. (2008). Detecting malingering in traumatic brain injury and chronic pain: A comparison of three forced-choice symptom validity tests. *The Clinical Neuropsychologist, 22*(5), 896–918.

Gruters, A. A., Ramakers, I. H., Verhey, F. R., Kessels, R. P., & de Vugt, M. E. (2021, pre-print). A scoping review of communicating neuropsychological test results to patients and family members. *Neuropsychol Rev.*

Hanson, S. L., Kerkhoff, T. R. (2018). Ethics in the practice of clinical neuropsychology: foundations and new horizons, in Kreutzer, J.S., DeLuca, J., & Caplan B. (Eds), *Encyclopedia of Clinical Neuropsychology.* Cham: Springer.

Harvey, P. D. (2012). Clinical applications of neuropsychological assessment. *Dialogues in Clinical Neuroscience, 14*(1), 91.

Hebben, N., & Milberg, W. (2009). *Essentials of Neuropsychological Assessment.* New York: John Wiley & Sons.

Hiscock, M. (2007). The Flynn Effect and its relevance to neuropsychology. *Journal of Clinical and Experimental Neuropsychology, 29*(5), 514–529.

Hula, W. et al. (2006). Rasch modeling of Revised Token Test Performance: Validity and sensitivity to change. *Journal of Speech, Language, and Hearing Research, 49*(1), 27–46.

Hustak, T., & Krejcar, O. (2016). Principles of usability in human-computer interaction, in Park, J., Chao, H. C., Arabnia, H., & Yen, N. (Eds), *Advanced Multimedia and Ubiquitous Engineering. Lecture Notes in Electrical Engineering,* vol. 354. Berlin & Heidelberg: Springer.

Huygelier, H., Gillebert, C. R., & Moors, P. (2021). The value of Bayesian methods for accurate and efficient neuropsychological assessment. *Journal of the International Neuropsychological Society,* 1–12.

ISTAT (2009). *La disabilità in Italia: il quadro della statistica ufficiale.* Roma: Sistema statistico nazionale.

Jacobson, N. S., & Truax P. (1991). Clinical significance: A statistical approach to defining meaningful change in psychotherapy research. *Journal of Consulting and Clinical Psychology, 59*(1), 12–19.

Jefferson, A. L., Paul, R. H., Ozonoff, A. L., & Cohen, R. A. (2006). Evaluating elements of executive functioning as predictors of instrumental activities of daily living (IADLs). *Archives of Clinical Neuropsychology, 21*(4), 311–320.

Jones-Gotman, M. (1991). Localization of lesions by neuropsychological testing. *Epilepsia, 32*(5), S41–52.

Kang, H., Zhao, F., You, L., Giorgetta, C., D, V., Sarkhel, S., & Prakash, R. (2014). Pseudo-dementia: A neuropsychological review. *Annals of Indian Academy of Neurology, 17*(2), 147–154.

Katz, S. et al. (1963). Studies of illness in the aged. The Index of ADL: A standardized measure of biological and psychosocial function. *Journal of the American Medical Association, 185*(12), 914–919.

Katzman, R., Terry, R., DeTeresa, R., Brown, T., Davies, P., Fuld, P., ... & Peck, A. (1988). Clinical, pathological, and neurochemical changes in dementia: A subgroup with preserved mental status and numerous neocortical plaques. *Annals of Neurology: Official Journal of the American Neurological Association and the Child Neurology Society, 23*(2), 138–144.

Kline, T. J. (2005). *Psychological Testing: A Practical Approach to Design and Evaluation.* Thousand Oaks, CA: Sage Publications.

Klinke, M. E., Hjaltason, H., Hafsteinsdóttir, T. B., & Jónsdóttir, H. (2016). Spatial neglect in stroke patients after discharge from rehabilitation to own home: A mixed method study. *Disability and Rehabilitation, 38*(25), 2429–2444.

Knol, A. S. L., Huiskes, M., Koole, T., Meganck, R., Loeys, T., & Desmet, M. (2020). Reformulating and mirroring in psychotherapy: A conversation analytic perspective. *Frontiers in Psychology, 11,* 318. doi:10.3389/fpsyg.2020.00318

Kouvari, M., D'Cunha, N. M., Travica, N., Sergi, D., Zec, M., Marx, W., & Naumovski, N. (2022). Metabolic syndrome, cognitive impairment and the role of diet: A narrative review. *Nutrients, 14,* 333.

Larrabee, G. J. (2012). A scientific approach to forensic neuropsychology, in Larrabee, G. J. (Ed.), *Forensic Neuropsychology: A Scientific Approach* (pp. 3–22). Oxford: Oxford University Press.

Lawshe, C. H. (1975). A quantitative approach to content validity. *Personnel Psychology, 28,* 563–575.

Lawton, M. P., & Brody, E. M. (1969). Assessment of older people: Self-maintaining and instrumental activities of daily living. *Gerontologist, 9*(1), 179–186.

Lezak, M. D., Howieson, D. B., Bigler, E. D., & Tranel, D. (2012). *Neuropsychological Assessment,* 5th edition. Oxford: Oxford University Press.

Lezak, M. D., Howieson, D. B., Loring, D. W., & Fischer, J. S. (2012). *Neuropsychological Assessment,* 5th edition. New York: Oxford University Press.

López-Franco, Ó., Morin, J. P., Cortés-Sol, A., Molina-Jiménez, T., Del Moral, D. I., Flores-Muñoz, M., Roldán-Roldán, G., Juárez-Portilla, C., & Zepeda, R. C. (2021). Cognitive impairment after resolution of hepatic encephalopathy: A systematic review and meta-analysis. *Frontiers in Neuroscience, 15,* 579263.

Luhmann, M., Hofmann, W., Eid, M., & Lucas, R. E. (2012). Subjective well-being and adaptation to life events: A meta-analysis. *Journal of Personality and Social Psychology, 102*(3), 592–615.

Martín-Rodríguez, J. F., & León-Carrión, J. (2010). Theory of mind deficits in patients with acquired brain injury: A quantitative review. *Neuropsychologia, 48*(5), 1181–1191.

Masina, F., Pezzetta, R., Lago, S., Mantini, D., Scarpazza, C., & Arcara, G. (2022). Disconnection from prediction: a systematic review on the role of right temporoparietal junction in aberrant predictive processing. *Neuroscience & Biobehavioral Reviews,* 104713.

Mast, M. S. (2007). On the importance of nonverbal communication in the physician-patient interaction. *Patient Education and Counseling, 67*(3), 315–318.

McCaffrey, R. J., & Westervelt, H. J. (1995). Issues associated with repeated neuropsychological assessments. *Neuropsychology Review, 5*(3), 203–221.

Menardi, A., Bertagnoni, G., Sartori, G., Pastore, M., & Mondini, S. (2020). Past life experiences and neurological recovery: The role of cognitive reserve in the rehabilitation of severe post-anoxic encephalopathy and traumatic brain injury. *Journal of the International Neuropsychological Society, 26*(4), 394–406.

Meng, X., & D'Arcy, C. (2012). Education and dementia in the context of the cognitive reserve hypothesis: a systematic review with meta-analyses and qualitative analyses. *PloS one, 7*(6), e38268.

Monaco, M., Costa, A., Caltagirone, C., & Carlesimo, G. A. (2013). Forward and backward span for verbal and visuo-spatial data: Standardization and normative data from an Italian adult population. *Neurological Sciences, 34*(5), 749–754.

Mondini, S. et al. (2011). *Esame Neuropsicologico breve-2. Una batteria di test per lo screening neuropsicologico*. Milano: Raffaello Cortina.

Mondini, S., Mapelli D., & Arcara G. (2015). *La valutazione neuropsicologica*. Roma: Carocci.

Mondini, S., Mapelli, D., & Arcara, G. (2016). *Semeiotica e diagnosi neuropsicologica: metodologia per la valutazione*. Roma; Carocci.

Montemurro, S., Daini, R., Tagliabue, C., Guzzetti, S., Gualco, G., Mondini, S., & Arcara, G. (2022). Cognitive reserve estimated with a life experience questionnaire outperforms education in predicting performance on MoCA: Italian normative data. *Current Psychology*, 1–15.

Mortamais, M., Ash, J. A., Harrison, J., Kaye, J., Kramer, J., Randolph, C., Pose, C., Albala, B., Ropacki, M., Ritchie, C. W., & Ritchie, K. (2017 April). Detecting cognitive changes in preclinical Alzheimer's disease: A review of its feasibility. *Alzheimers Dement., 13*(4), 468–492.

Murphy, M. J., & Peterson, M. J. (2015). Sleep disturbances in depression. *Sleep Medicine Clinics, 10*(1), 17–23.

Nasreddine, Z. S., Phillips, N. A., Bédirian, V., Charbonneau, S., Whitehead, V., Collin, I., Cummings, J. L., & Chertkow, H. (2005 April). The Montreal Cognitive Assessment, MoCA: A brief screening tool for mild cognitive impairment. *J. Am. Geriatr. Soc., 53*(4), 695–699. doi:10.1111/j.1532-5415.2005.53221.x

Nelson, H. E., & Willison, J. (1991). *National adult reading test (NART)*. Windsor: NFER-Nelson.

Norris, G., & Tate, R. L. (2000). The Behavioural Assessment of the Dysexecutive Syndrome (BADS): Ecological, concurrent and construct validity. *Neuropsychological Rehabilitation, 10*(1), 33–45.

Nucci, M., Mapelli, D., & Mondini, S. (2012). Cognitive Reserve Index questionnaire (CRIq): A new instrument for measuring cognitive reserve. *Aging Clinical and Experimental Research, 24*(3), 218–226.

O'Connell, M. E., Tuokko, H., & Kadlec, H. (2011). Demographic corrections appear to compromise classification accuracy for severely skewed cognitive tests. *Journal of Clinical and Experimental Neuropsychology, 33*(4), 422–431.

Ouvrard, C., Berr, C., Meillon, C., Ribet, C., Goldberg, M., Zins, M., & Amieva, H. (2019). Norms for standard neuropsychological tests from the French CONSTANCES cohort. *European Journal of Neurology, 26*(5), 786–793.

Pedraza, O., & Mungas, D. (2008). Measurement in cross-cultural neuropsychology. *Neuropsychology Review, 18*(3), 184–193.

Perini, G., Cotta Ramusino, M., Sinforiani, E., Bernini, S., Petrachi, R., & Costa, A. (2019). Cognitive impairment in depression: Recent advances and novel treatments. *Neuropsychiatric Disease and Treatment, 15*, 1249–1258.

Peterson, R. T., & Limbu, Y. (2009). The convergence of mirroring and empathy: Communications training in business-to-business personal selling persuasion efforts. *Journal of Business-To-Business Marketing, 16*(3), 193–219.

Pezzullo, L. (2002). Cheating neuropsychologists: A study of cognitive processes involved in scientific anomalies resolution. *Mind & Society, 3*(1), 43–50.

Pimental, P. A., O'Hara, J. B., Jandak, J. L. (2018). Neuropsychologists as primary care providers of cognitive health: A novel comprehensive cognitive wellness service delivery model. *Appl. Neuropsychol. Adult, 25*(4), 318–326.

Pinto, E., & Peters, R. (2009). Literature review of the Clock Drawing Test as a tool for cognitive screening. *Dementia and Geriatric Cognitive Disorders, 27*(3), 201–213.

Pirani, A., Nasreddine, Z. S., Tulipani, C., & Neri, M. (2007). Montreal Cognitive Assessment (MOCA): Uno strumento rapido per lo screening del Mild Cognitive Impairment, in *Dati preliminari della versione italiana. Atti IV Congresso Regionale Associazione Italiana Psicogeriatria, Bologna.*

Pirau, L., & Lui, F. (2021). *Frontal Lobe Syndrome.* StatPearls Publishing.

Pirrotta, F., Timpano, F., Bonanno, L., Nunnari, D., Marino, S., Bramanti, P., & Lanzafame, P. (2015). Italian validation of Montreal Cognitive Assessment. *European Journal of Psychological Assessment, 1*(2), 131–137.

Pitteri, M., Arcara, G., Passarini, L., Meneghello, F., & Priftis, K. (2013). Is two better than one? Limb activation treatment combined with contralesional arm vibration to ameliorate signs of left neglect. *Frontiers in Human Neuroscience, 7*, 460.

Poldrack, R. A., & Yarkoni, T. (2016). From brain maps to cognitive ontologies: informatics and the search for mental structure. *Annual Review of Psychology, 67*, 587–612.

Poletti, M., Enrici, I., & Adenzato, M. (2012). Cognitive and affective theory of mind in neurodegenerative diseases: neuropsychological, neuroanatomical and neurochemical levels. *Neuroscience & Biobehavioral Reviews, 36*(9), 2147–2164.

Ponsford, J. (Ed.) (2004). *Cognitive and Behavioral Rehabilitation: From Neurobiology to Clinical Practice.* New York: Guilford Press.

Pool, L. R., Weuve, J., Wilson, R. S., Bültmann, U., Evans, D. A., & Mendes de Leon, C. F. (2016). Occupational cognitive requirements and late-life cognitive aging. *Neurology, 86*(15), 1386–1392.

Prieto, G. et al. (2010). Scoring neuropsychological tests using the Rasch Model: An illustrative example with the Rey-Osterrieth Complex Figure. *The Clinical Neuropsychologist, 24*(1), 45–56.

Reitan, R. M. (1958), Validity of Trail Making Test as an indicator of organic brain damage. *Perceptual and Motor Skills, 8*, 193–198.

Rao, S. M. (1990). The Cognitive Function Study Group of the National Multiple Sclerosis Society. *A Manual for the Brief Repeatable Battery of Neuropsychological Tests in Multiple Sclerosis.*

Raven, J. C. (2008). *SPM Standard Progressive Matrices. Standardizzazione italiana [Italian standardization]*. Firenze: Giunti OS.

Reed, J. C., & Reed, H. B. (1997). The Halstead-Reitan Neuropsychological Battery, in Reed, J. C., & Reed, H. B., *Contemporary Approaches to Neuropsychological Assessment* (pp. 93–129). Boston, MA: Springer.

Riddoch, M., & Humphreys, G. W. (1994). *Cognitive Neuropsychology and Cognitive Rehabilitation*. New York: Lawrence Erlbaum Associates, Inc.

Robin, T. Peterson & Yam Limbu (2009). The convergence of mirroring and empathy: Communications training in business-to-business personal selling persuasion efforts. *Journal of Business-to-Business Marketing, 16*(3), 193–219.

Rosenich, E., Hordacre, B., Paquet, C., Koblar, S. A., & Hillier, S. L. (2020). Cognitive reserve as an emerging concept in stroke recovery. *Neurorehabilitation and Neural Repair, 34*(3), 187–199.

Rousseaux, M., Daveluy, W., & Kozlowski, O. (2010). Communication in conversation in stroke patients. *Journal of Neurology, 257*(7), 1099–1107.

Russell, E. W. (2011). *The Scientific Foundation of Neuropsychological Assessment: With Applications to Forensic Evaluation*. Amsterdam & Boston: Elsevier.

Salinsky, M. C., Storzbach, D., Dodrill, C. B., & Binder, L. M. (2001). Test–retest bias, reliability, and regression equations for neuropsychological measures repeated over a 12–16-week period. *Journal of the International Neuropsychological Society, 7*(5), 597–605.

Salvadori, E., Pasi, M., Poggesi, A., Chiti, G., Inzitari, D., & Pantoni, L. (2013). Predictive value of MoCA in the acute phase of stroke on the diagnosis of mid-term cognitive impairment. *Journal of Neurology, 260*(9), 2220–2227.

Santangelo, G., Siciliano, M., Pedone, R., Vitale, C., Falco, F., Bisogno, R., ... & Trojano, L. (2015). Normative data for the Montreal Cognitive Assessment in an Italian population sample. *Neurological Sciences, 36*(4), 585–591.

Semenza, C., Meneghello, F., Arcara, G., Burgio, F., Gnoato, F., Facchini, S., ... & Butterworth, B. (2014). A new clinical tool for assessing numerical abilities in neurological diseases: numerical activities of daily living. *Frontiers in Aging Neuroscience, 6*, 112.

Slick, D. J. (2006a). Psychometric in neuropsychological assessment, in Strauss E., Sherman E. M., & Spreen O. (2006). *A Compendium of Neuropsychological Tests: Administration, Norms, and Commentary* (pp. 3–43). New York: Oxford University Press.

Slick, D. J. (2006b). Norms selection in neuropsychological assessment, in Strauss E., Sherman E. M., & Spreen O. (2006). *A Compendium of Neuropsychological Tests: Administration, Norms, and Commentary* (pp. 44–54). New York: Oxford University Press.

Spinnler, H., & Tognoni, G. (1987). Standardizzazione e taratura italiana di test neuropsicologici. *Italian Journal of Neurological Sciences, 8*(6), 1–20.

Stern, Y. (2009). Cognitive reserve. *Neuropsychologia, 47*(10), 2015–2028.

Stevens, S. S. (1946). On the theory of scales of measurement. *Science, 103*(2684), 677–680.

Steward, K. A., Kennedy, R., Novack, T. A., Crowe, M., Marson, D. C., & Triebel, K. L. (2018). The role of cognitive reserve in recovery from traumatic brain injury. *The Journal of Head Trauma Rehabilitation, 33*(1), E18–E27.

Stimmel, M., Shagalow, S., Seng, E. K., Portnoy, J. G., Archetti, R., Mendelowitz, E. et al. (2019). Short report: Adherence to neuropsychological recommendations in patients with multiple sclerosis. *The International Journal of MS Care*, *21*(2), 70–75.

Stone, M. H., Wright, B. D., & Stenner, A. J. (1999). Mapping variables. *Journal of Outcome Measurement*, *3*, 308–322.

Strauss, E., Sherman, E. M., & Spreen, O. (2006). *A Compendium of Neuropsychological Tests: Administration, Norms, and Commentary*. New York: Oxford University Press.

Strong, M. J., Abrahams, S., Goldstein, L. H., Woolley, S., Mclaughlin, P., Snowden, J., ... & Turner, M. R. (2017). Amyotrophic lateral sclerosis-frontotemporal spectrum disorder (ALS-FTSD): Revised diagnostic criteria. *Amyotrophic Lateral Sclerosis and Frontotemporal Degeneration*, *18*(3–4), 153–174.

Sun, W., Matsuoka, T., Oba, H., & Narumoto, J. (2021). Importance of loneliness in behavioral and psychological symptoms of dementia. *International Journal of Geriatric Psychiatry*, *36*(4), 540–546.

Thomann, A. E., Goettel, N., Monsch, R. J., Berres, M., Jahn, T., Steiner, L. A., & Monsch, A. U. (2018). The Montreal Cognitive Assessment: Normative data from a German-speaking cohort and comparison with international normative samples. *Journal of Alzheimer's Disease*, *64*(2), 643–655.

Thomas, M. L., Brown, G. G., Gur, R. C., Moore, T. M., Patt, V. M., Risbrough, V. B., & Baker, D. G. (2018). A signal detection–item response theory model for evaluating neuropsychological measures. *Journal of Clinical and Experimental Neuropsychology*, *40*(8), 745–760.

Trachsel, M., Hermann, H., & Biller-Andorno, N. (2015). Cognitive fluctuations as a challenge for the assessment of decision-making capacity in patients with dementia. *American Journal of Alzheimer's Disease & Other Dementias*, *30*(4), 360–363.

Trizano-Hermosilla, I., & Alvarado, J. M. (2016). Best alternatives to Cronbach's alpha reliability in realistic conditions: Congeneric and asymmetrical measurements. *Frontiers in Psychology*, *7*, 769. University Press.

Urbina, S. (2004). *Essentials of Psychological Testing*. New York: Wiley.

Voutilainen, L., and Peräkylä, A. (2014). Therapeutic conversation, in Östman, J.-O., & Verschueren, J. (Eds), *Handbook of Pragmatics*. Amsterdam: John Benjamins.

Wade, D. T. (2020). What is rehabilitation? An empirical investigation leading to an evidence-based description. *Clinical Rehabilitation*, *34*(5), 571–583.

Watt, S., & Crowe, S. F. (2018). Examining the beneficial effect of neuropsychological assessment on adult patient outcomes: a systematic review. *The Clinical Neuropsychologist*, *32*(3), 368–390.

Wechsler, D. (1939). *The Measurement of Adult Intelligence*. Baltimore: Williams & Witkins.

White, R. F., & Rose, F. E. (1997). The Boston process approach, in White, R. F., & Rose, F. E., *Contemporary Approaches to Neuropsychological Assessment* (pp. 171–211). Boston, MA: Springer.

Williams, R. L. (2013). Overview of the Flynn Effect. *Intelligence*, *41*(6), 753–764.

Wilson, B. A. (2008). Neuropsychological rehabilitation. *Annual Review of Clinical Psychology*, *4*(1), 141–162.

Zanin, E., Aiello, E. N., Diana, L., Fusi, G., Bonato, M., Niang, A., Ognibene, F., Corvaglia, A., De Caro, C., Cintoli, S., Marchetti, G., Vestri, A., & Italian working group on tele-neuropsychology (TELA) (2022). Tele-neuropsychological assessment tools in Italy: a systematic review on psychometric properties and usability. *Neurological Sciences: official journal of the Italian Neurological Society and of the Italian Society of Clinical Neurophysiology, 43*(1), 125–138.

Zilliox, L. A., Chadrasekaran, K., Kwan, J. Y., & Russell, J. W. (2016). Diabetes and cognitive impairment. *Current Diabetes Reports, 16*(9), 87.

Index